PRAISE FOR
Transforming Libraries

"I have had the good fortune of watching Ron Starker in action at the Singapore American School and his library is electric! His book is a must-read."

—CHRIS CRUTCHER, author of
The Crazy Horse Electric Game

"*Transforming Libraries* offers a revolutionary approach for libraries of the future. This is a crucial and timely book."

—YING COMPESTINE, author of
Revolution is Not a Dinner Party

"Standing in the middle school library at the Singapore American School is something of a fantasy. Students, faculty, and staff are all engaged in a variety of exercises, tutorials, conversations, activities, and even workshops, in a way that exemplifies what a modern library should be. Having visited Ron's library many times, I can honestly say that I have never been to the same place twice. The space is constantly changing, adapting, and thriving in a way that creates a buzzing energy, educational nourishment, and a feeling of home. As the role of the library is starting to be questioned in an ever-evolving world, Ron Starker's *Transforming Libraries* provides an effective blueprint for the library space revolution that is coming our way. A must-read!"

—SEAN THOMAS, anchor/correspondent for
International News Channel RT

"With an ever-present sense of humor, Ron Starker provides innovative and truly practical ideas for transforming school libraries into dynamic, living, learning spaces. While advocating for continually developing a library with pioneering and diverse learning tools to touch each and every learner, Ron has not discounted the importance of 'traditional' library tools (i.e. quiet, reflective spaces, print books in additional to digital resources) as a valuable component of a transformed library."

—JENNA EMERSON FOLLET, senior educational consultant

"*Transforming Libraries* is an onslaught of ideas for taking what may be quiet and dusty and turning it into inspiringly active. Starker looks at an expansive variety of possibilities for the evolving library and provides examples, links, and no small portion of humor to engage a reader excited about what a school's library can be. Toward the end, he explores the difference between the 'talker' and the 'doer,' and this book is very much a guide for the latter."

—RUSHTON HURLEY, Executive Director of NextVista.org and
author of *Making Your School Something Special*

"My children and I thoroughly enjoyed our visit to this library. While surrounded by wonderful books, we played musical instruments and gazed at 3D images. The experience created a sense of excitement about the possibilities of learning in this type of setting."

—DR. PETER ESO, Oxford University,
Department of Economics

"*Transforming Libraries* is insightful, thought provoking, and humorous. Librarians who lack money or space for innovative changes will find many useful ideas worth adopting."

—TERRI ROLFE, secondary school
librarian, Vienna, Austria

Transforming Libraries

A TOOLKIT FOR INNOVATORS, MAKERS, AND SEEKERS

Ron Starker

*grafo*EDU

Bothell, Washington, USA
Guadalajara, Jalisco, Mexico

Transforming Libraries
© 2017 by Ron Starker

Published by Grafo Education

Grafo Education is an imprint of Grafo House Publishing
In association with Jaquith Creative, a literary and creative agency
grafohouse.com / jaquithcreative.com
Originally published by EdTechTeam Press

Printed edition ISBN: 978-1-949791-09-9
Ebook edition ISBN: 978-1-949791-10-5
Library of Congress Control Number: 2019916604

This book is available at special discounts when purchased in quantity for use as premiums, promotions, fundraising, and educational use. For inquiries and details, contact the publisher at info@grafohouse.com

Printed in the United States of America
23 22 21 20 19   1 2 3 4 5

To my wife, Kate Bucknall,
who gives me all of my best ideas.

Contents

Preface

Most adolescents today are highly involved in the world of social media. Teens and 'tweens are seeking to understand themselves and one another through postings on multiple digital platforms. This is happening at a time in their development that psychologist Erik Erikson defines as the stage of "identity vs. role confusion." Forming one's identity is far more complex today, than it was when Erikson did his research in the 1960s and 70s. Our use of social media now allows us to create multiple digital identities.

Currently, a gap exists between the way we conduct education and the way students go about their personal learning. Schools and universities have not really caught up with technology. Cultural anthropologist Michael Welsch PhD at Kansas State University illustrates this gap in his video, "A Vision of Students Today," the contrast is both striking and disturbing. In another video titled "Learning to Change—Changing to Learn," Keith Krueger, CEO of The Consortium of School Networking, says, "When fifty-five sectors of the economy were analyzed for technological sophistication, schools ranked fifty-fifth, just behind coal mining." Libraries are in a unique position to bridge this gap and to help individuals cope with the rewards and challenges that new technologies place upon all of us.

THE TIPPING POINT

Simply put, today's libraries are in jeopardy. In *The Tipping Point*, author Malcolm Gladwell illustrates how the demand for change often reaches a tipping point, until a whole cascade of changes suddenly begins. School libraries are approaching that tipping point.

Many people believe libraries are no longer necessary or even viable in today's digital age, creating a compelling argument for the Internet, and subsequently, e-books, as replacements. After all, why do we need libraries when we have Google? A similar argument was made in the sixties, when advertisements stating microfiche readers in homes would end the need for libraries.

The difference, though, is that today, the concept of book warehouses is in jeopardy, while the concept of libraries as gathering points for collaboration, innovation, and authentic learning is only just beginning to take shape. Libraries transformed into innovation centers are the perfect settings for implementing change within a school or community. Adapting to exponential growth in knowledge is not a matter of running faster or working harder—we will never keep up. Instead, it's a matter of working smarter.

It's Time for a Makeover

If, like me, you are a librarian, you have to acknowledge we have an image problem. Stereotypes form as a kind of shorthand for understanding the world, and they always contain an element of truth along with inaccurate generalizations. That said, libraries are viewed as outdated, and librarians are frequently seen as rigid and humorless.

Ask children to draw a picture of a scientist, and you will probably get a rough image of Einstein in his later years. Ask these same children to draw a librarian, and they'll draw someone who looks a bit like Marge Simpson and acts like one of her cynical sisters. The first line of the "Librarians in popular culture" Wikipedia article sums this up well by saying, "Stereotypes of librarians in popular culture are frequently negative: librarians are portrayed as puritanical, punitive, unattractive, and introverted if female, or timid and effeminate if male." Ouch! We need a complete makeover.

Terri Rolfe posing as a stereotypical librarian.

Case in point: my good friend Terri Rolfe, the American International School (AIS) of Vienna's high school librarian, demonstrates this kind of makeover in her AIS Vienna Library Orientation video by making fun of the librarian stereotype and performing some of the cool gymnastic moves she taught as a coach.[1]

Like Terri, librarians should transform from gatekeepers into innovators and entrepreneurs. Likewise, libraries need to shift from simply warehouses storing information into centers of innovation and experimentation. Now, I realize these ideas are not new, and many of today's librarians are already doing elements of what I am proposing. However, I know many of the ideas in this book will prove a challenge to the old guard (some quite young) who want to maintain libraries as comfortable centers for quiet contemplation and reflection, without ever addressing society's broader needs. For this makeover to be successful, though, we must find ways to preserve the best elements of libraries and librarianship that work well, while discarding and changing ineffective, outdated practices.

---

1   Watch the video here: http://bit.ly/2hijUmz.

Terri Rolfe, Librarian at AIS Vienna

THIS IS NO LAUGHING MATTER, OR IS IT?

Let me preface this section by stating that understanding the nature of informational sources is fundamental to evaluating the truth and validity of what we're told. (Full disclosure: I am not a professor of library and information science, nor do I feel bound by rigid institutional or theoretical constraints. And while I'm passionate about libraries and the ideas in this book, I realize I don't have even half the answers to the challenges libraries are facing today, nor does anyone else, for that matter.)

As librarians, we need to laugh more, and we need to laugh at ourselves and at the crazy situations we find ourselves in from time to time. We need to start trying radical, or at least new, ideas. Only then will we ever break the negative stereotypes. Librarians can be a bit too serious, so I want to add a bit of levity to the discussion. Yes, our work is important, but we rarely face the pressures of a surgeon performing open-heart surgery, the conflicts of a police officer making an arrest, or the stress of a pilot landing a plane carrying hundreds of passengers. Losing a few thousand MARC records can never compete with these stresses. I believe humor is life affirming and adds to our creativity, so, fair warning, I will be introducing middle school, low-grade humor into the mix, just to remind us that if we get it wrong, it won't be the end of the world. Too often, libraries are seen as somewhere you should never laugh, like a church. Make no mistake, this is a frontal assault on that attitude.

WELCOME TO THE REVOLUTION

If you are interested in the world of information and how we access, curate, and create information, you will find this book useful. If you view yourself as an innovator or change agent, this book is for you. If you are a bit of a revolutionary, even better.

As I will stress throughout these pages, for schools and libraries to function more effectively in tomorrow's world, we need to consider radical changes. While this book is mainly intended for school librarians, I hope these ideas might also be read and considered by technology coordinators, teachers, students, and school administrators. As with any educational effort, though, I realize, ultimately, teachers are key. Because only when we enlist teachers will school libraries become dynamic. But instead of expecting teachers to take on yet another job, we need to facilitate and help teachers as they, too, transform their job roles and work. Together, we must take into account the interests and passions of the students who enter our shared space and foster meaningful connections within and beyond our school's curriculum.

As you'll see, I have consulted with "thought partners" from a variety of settings and job roles, and I will nudge you into questioning traditional viewpoints and encourage you to consider the school library as a catalyst for educational change.

In the thirty-five years I've worked in educational settings, I've learned schools are among the slowest institutions to change. As technology evolves at an exponential speed, schools are left struggling to cope. I have collaborated with students in middle school, high school, college, and graduate school, and in every setting, change moves in a slow, gradual upward spiral. But, today, outside influences in the forms of technology and societal change seem poised to alter our current situation in a dramatic fashion.

School libraries offer space, tools, informational resources, and staff not otherwise available in the classroom. Libraries are the perfect setting for trying new ideas and innovations. They can serve as centers for research and development, whether through individual endeavor, cross-disciplinary study, or collaborative group work. And no matter if you are a librarian, an administrator, a student, or a teacher, the library belongs to you—you need to play a role in determining how library staff and resources can be best used within your school or community.

THE ROAD TO SHAMBHALA

Over many centuries, numerous explorers and seekers of spiritual wisdom have embarked on expeditions and quests in search of the mythical paradise of Shambhala....
—*from "Mysteries of the Kingdom of Shambhala," OSHO News*

Typically, a book like this one studies best practices from a range of settings so as to paint a portrait of the "ideal," or what the reader should strive to emulate. While I have visited many public, school, and academic libraries around the world, most of what I offer is based on one case study alone: the Singapore American School Middle School Library, where I just happen to work.

We are set within an urban, English-speaking environment in Singapore on a prekindergarten through twelfth-grade campus educating nearly 4,000 students. Our middle school library serves ninety-five faculty members and 950 middle school students. The school's student body is approximately 65 percent American, with students and faculty representing more than sixty other countries. Our library encompasses approximately 1,100 square meters on one floor. Now, by no means is our library perfect, nor has everything the staff and I have tried worked well, but we have created a popular, vibrant space while also having fun trying to personalize and individualize a highly diverse population's learning experiences. I am not talking about a hypothetical situation; rather, my colleagues and I have tried and tested almost every idea presented in this book.

It is tempting to look for the "perfect school" or the "perfect library," the utopia, Shangri-La, or, in the words of author Garrison Keillor, the "Lake Wobegon, where all the women are strong, all the men are good looking, and all the children are above average." But there is no perfect library, no perfect school, no perfect setting for learning, no Shambhala—we have to create it, watch it disappear, and then create it again.

As part of my school's quest to develop the best learning programs, we have visited a fair number of "top schools" in America, and I can assure you, no one place has it all. So, if you are seeking to visit the "best library" or "the best school," save your money and start building it right where you are. In an article titled "Valley Visitors Must Bring Back More Than the T-Shirt," Financial Times West Coast editor Richard Waters writes that he's found "pilgrimages to innovation centers often amount to nothing more than 'innovation tourism,' as it is difficult to inject ideas and models into new settings without first planting the seeds for the harvest."

What's more, the Chinese say the monks in the temple are not as good as the ones outside, and I agree—you need the confidence to listen to colleagues whom you admire and respect and to seek out experts within your own setting. If you want ideas from experts, then read books, blogs, and websites. And if you really want to learn how something works, try having a Skype session with the expert (and maybe even offer to compensate them for their time) so you can better use your time and money to develop solutions customized to meet your library's challenges.

WE ARE ALL IN THE SAME SPEEDBOAT

When you think about it, libraries aren't the only institutions in for a big shock—all of our institutions are facing radical changes. Doctors are increasingly faced with patients who have done extensive research on specialty topics prior to consultations. Journalists are facing stiff competition from crowdsourced information, further blurring the lines between professional journalism and social commentary. Schools are seeing an increasingly greater share of learning taking place outside the classroom. Our movements, conversations, locations, shopping habits, interests, and social transactions are being captured through credit cards, ATM machines, GPS devices, video cams, sensors, and digital media more frequently and casually than ever before. Machines and artificial intelligence, once fodder for science-fiction novels and movies, are entering our world in the form of robotics, nanotechnology, and the Internet. Globalization and the threats of climate change are leaving us more interdependent than ever before, but our political mechanisms are still largely creations of previous centuries. In short, almost every institution and occupation as we currently know it will be affected by both this knowledge and technology revolution.

As librarians, we can choose to either be cast aside as relics, or we can step up to the challenges before us and provide relevant tools, learning spaces, and opportunities for creative solutions to emerge. Libraries can either serve as lifeboats or space shuttles on this grand journey—it's our decision.

CHAPTER 1

The Best of Times

It was the best of times, it was the worst of times, it was the age of wisdom, it was the age of foolishness, it was the epoch of belief, it was the epoch of incredulity, it was the season of Light, it was the season of Darkness, it was the spring of hope, it was the winter of despair, we had everything before us, we had nothing before us.

—**Charles Dickens,** A Tale of Two Cities

Dickens' introduction in *A Tale of Two Cities* bears some semblance to the current situation we librarians are finding ourselves in. That's because, for so many of us, we really are living in the best of times for libraries—more books are in print than ever before, there are more libraries than ever before, and more people are using libraries than ever before. Yet a growing chorus believe libraries have reached a tipping point, and quite possibly, the point of no return.

Many serious and well-informed forecasters believe the extinction of libraries is on the horizon. Yet despite economic collapse, natural disasters, raids by barbarians, countless inventions, cultural revolutions, terrorism, wars, and any number of other threats over the past three millennia, libraries have managed to not only survive—they've flourished. Writing this book is my small contribution to supporting the transformation of, and thereby, survival of, libraries. We cannot afford to lose one of civilization's most valuable assets. We need libraries to help us to create a better future.

GREAT LIBRARIES OF THE WORLD

We can take heart in knowing some of the most incredible examples of public and academic libraries around the world have survived the centuries. You'll find these temples of knowledge housed within the most spectacular architectural creations known to man. One empire after another has seen the need to establish remarkable settings to document and capture the knowledge of each age, from the ancient Egyptians, to the Greeks and Romans in the West, to the Indian subcontinent and the great Chinese, Japanese, and Korean cultures in the East. It's not simply a matter of chance that libraries have played a significant role in preserving and furthering the development of civilization. Each culture designed their libraries to safeguard the power, riches, and wisdom it held as sacrosanct. One must hope mathematician and physicist Isaac Newton was in a library, or at least standing on several stacks of books at the time, when he noted that, "If I have seen further than others, it is by standing on the shoulders of giants."

Although most libraries from the ancient world are now in ruins, what remains of them tells us part of their cultures' stories. Case in point: Turkey's Library of Celsus (AD 135) in Ephesus, the Library of Pergamum (circa 197-60 BCE) in Bergama, and Egypt's original Library of Alexandria. Through stunning photography and vivid language, architectural historian James W.P. Campbell and photographer Will Pryce beautifully document what remains of some of these libraries in their book, *The Library: A World History*. Fortunately, a few now function both as museums as well as centers for scholarly research. In

Figure 1.1, you'll find examples of great libraries dating as far back as the sixteenth century that are still in existence. (Note: This list is by no means a ranking. In fact, I have left out many of the world's most famous libraries.)

LIBRARIES THROUGH THE CENTURIES

Fifteenth Century Libraries
Queens College Library: 1448, Cambridge, UK

Sixteenth-Century Libraries
Biblioteca Marciana: 1584, Venice, Italy
Merton College Library: 1589, Oxford, UK

Seventeenth-Century Libraries
Biblioteca Ambrosiana: 1609, Milan
Bodleian Library: 1612, Oxford, UK
Theological Hall Strahov Abbey: 1679, Prague, Czech Republic

Eighteenth-Century Libraries
Herzog August Bibliothek: 1710, Wolfenbüttel, Germany
Hofbibliothek: 1730, Vienna, Austria
Biblioteca Angelica: 1765, Rome, Italy
Mafra Palace Library: 1771, Mafra, Portugal
Biblioteca Palafoxiana: 1772, Puebla, Mexico

Nineteenth-Century Libraries
Trinity College Library: 1856, Dublin, Ireland
The George Peabody Library: 1866, Baltimore, Maryland, USA

Twentieth-Century Libraries
Osaka Library: 1904, Osaka, Japan
National Library of Brazil: 1910, Rio de Janeiro
NY Public Library: 1911, New York City
Russian State Library: 1945, Moscow
The Beinecke Library: 1963, New Haven, Connecticut, USA

Figure 1.1 Source: *The Library: A World History*

Among the greatest libraries still standing is the American Library of Congress, which earns the title of the largest library in the world. Housing more than 160 million items, including thirty-four million books, the Library of Congress is an impressive showcase and important research hub for both American and world culture and history.

Library of Congress

Equally impressive is London's British Library, with 150 million items and 16,000 people using the collections on-site and online each day. The library houses treasures from the British Empire and ancient civilizations, including some of the most valuable maps and treaties on Earth.

British Library

This tendency for empires to want to capture their knowledge and culture through libraries extends to the world of education as well.

Most of the world's top universities and schools have built amazing libraries to emphasize their focus on learning. In fact, a school's library is one of the most common features that parents and students look at when choosing a school.

THE UNITED STATES' TEN LARGEST LIBRARY BOOK COLLECTIONS

Library of Congress	34,528,818
Boston Public Library	19,090,261
Harvard University	16,832,952
New York Public Library	16,342,365
University of Illinois-Urbana/Champaign	13,158,748
Yale University	12,787,962
University of California-Berkeley	11,545,418
Columbia University	11,189,036
University of Michigan	10,778,736
University of Texas-Austin	9,990,941

Figure 1.2   *Source: American Library Association*

Just as it is critical that we save the ruins of libraries past, it is equally imperative that we preserve today's incredible buildings and their historical collections for generations to come. Digitization of collections is highly valuable, but we also need to retain the physical artifacts of books and other manuscripts to fully understand and appreciate the context of their ideas. Luckily, we can do just this, all the while creating new types of libraries to serve us today and tomorrow—it's not an either-or situation. We do not need to follow the barbarians' lead and try to destroy the great libraries of civilization; rather, we can have all sorts of libraries and library hybrids in our future while still respecting the past. Great libraries are not limited to relics—new libraries with a sense of modern grandeur and state-of-the-art technology are being built each year.

NOTEWORTHY EXAMPLES OF LIBRARIES OF THE MODERN ERA

Bibliothèque Nationale: 1996, Paris, France

Tu Delft Library: 1997, Delft, Netherlands

Shiba Ryotaro Museum: 2001, Osaka, Japan

Utrecht University Library: 2004, Utrecht, Netherlands

José Vasconcelos Library: 2006, Mexico City, Mexico

Tama Art University: 2007, Tokyo, Japan

The National Library of China: 2008, Beijing, China

The Grimm Center: 2009, Berlin, Germany

The Liyuan Library: 2012, Jiaojiehe, China

Figure 1.3   *Source: The Library: A World History*

This is all great, but aside from these showcase libraries, how are the thousands of other libraries around the world doing? Are people still frequenting libraries, and are libraries worth the cost? According to the Online Computer Library Center (OCLC), the United States has an impressive number of libraries that are patronized by huge numbers of people. (See Figure 1.4 on page 8.) That said, the OCLC numbers also indicate that libraries in the Western world are starting to decline in number, while Asia is experiencing significant growth. Experts say the most likely reason for these shifts is Asia's economic boom and the West's economic decline.

What do we see in number from the United States? Well, schools overwhelmingly have more libraries and librarians. Academic libraries have far more books. Public libraries have far more patrons, and special libraries have a lot more of everything than I personally ever expected.

According to the U.S. Census Bureau, the population of the United States currently (2017) stands at 324 million people. Based on the OCLC statistics cited in Figure 1.4, the United States has a total of 103,641 libraries storing 2,505,713,485 books and other informational items. To put this in perspective, this means there is one library for every 3,197 citizens in America. As of 2017, most of the information contained in books was available only in print form and has not yet been digitized or placed on the Internet. The amount of other information available online vastly outweighs these large numbers.

IT TAKES ALL TYPES

Libraries tend to fall into the four major categories:

- **Academic**—Serve the staff, students, and faculty of colleges and universities

- **Public**—Serve communities of all sizes, types, and patrons of all ages

- **School**—Serve students ranging in age from kindergarten through twelfth grade to more specialized high schools, middle schools, intermediate schools, and primary schools in public and private settings

- **Special**—Operate within specialized environments, including, but not limited to: corporations, hospitals, museums, governmental agencies, and legal firms

LIBRARIES
IN THE UNITED STATES

Academic
(2012)
3,793 libraries
26,606 librarians
7,641,610 users
1,099,951,212 books

Public
(2013)
9,042 libraries
47,500 librarians
170,911,558 users
776,682,289 books

School
(2008)
81,920 libraries
59,760 librarians
48,700,000 users
399,918,034 books

Special
(2008)
6,590 libraries
21,172 librarians
1,525,619 users
229,161,950 books

TOTAL

101,345 libraries

155,038 librarians

228,778,787 users

2,505,713,485 books

Figure 1.4   *Source: Online Computer Library Center*

The American Library Association (ALA), which serves all categories of libraries, outlines these librarian job specialties on their website to show the breadth of the profession:

- Aquatic and marine science librarians
- Archivists
- Art librarians
- Bookmobile and outreach librarians
- Children's services librarians
- Film librarians
- Government documents librarians
- Law librarians
- Map and geography librarians
- Medical librarians
- Music librarians
- Prison librarians
- Reference librarians
- Science librarians
- Substance abuse librarians
- Theatre librarians
- Theological librarians
- Youth services librarians

The top-rated graduate programs in library and information studies are listed by *U.S. News and World Report*. This list shows the specialty areas currently offered in their programs:

- Archives and preservation
- Digital librarianship
- Health librarianship
- Information systems
- Law librarianship
- School library media
- Services for children and youth

HYBRIDS, MASH-UPS, AND REMIXES ARE ALL POSSIBLE

The ALA's list of job specialties and the *U.S. News and World Report's* library school specialty areas all look a bit old-fashioned. Actually, on second thought, they look hopelessly antiquated. Libraries have to better address the changing needs of their patrons and communities; they need to provide more than simply access to information. They must facilitate learning and help members to create new content whether it is in the form of books, videos, musical compositions, graphical design, or any forms of innovative endeavor.

Here is an alternative list of specialty areas that I feel need to be employed by our schools of library and information science:

- *Creative content developers*

- *Digital management specialists*

- *Emerging technology librarians*

- *Gaming specialists*

- *Learning design specialists*

- *Makerspace librarians*

Librarians trained in the specialities listed above need to work alongside other professionals who can help patrons with their learning needs. Specialists such as audio technicians, videographers, artists and designers, carpenters, engineers, literacy coaches, counselors, computer programmers, artificial intelligence specialists, robotics engineers, software developers, fitness coaches, and visiting speakers and presenters all assist in the creation of a dynamic learning and innovation center, the library of the future.

THE VIRTUAL LIBRARY

Since the early days of the Internet, and more specifically, the worldwide web, newspaper and magazine articles have been announcing that libraries are becoming a thing of the past. Commentators have been arguing for years that a comprehensive virtual library will replace printed books and lead to the closing of brick-and-mortar libraries. After all, they say, in the not-too-distant future, we will have all the informational sources we need delivered right to our mobile devices. Indeed, we are living in exciting times, and by no means am I a Luddite seeking to block such technologies, but I think it's important to separate the facts from the hyperbole.

Each time a new communication medium or format is developed, people begin assuming the older format will disappear. Forty-five short play records were replaced by thirty-three LPs, which, in turn, were replaced by cassettes, CDs, DVDs, and now MP3s. Yet, many older formats have survived simply because they possess unique features. For example, people predicted radio would disappear when TV arrived, yet today, radio is thriving right alongside its old rival.

But now, with the blistering pace of technology, it seems reasonable to assume The Google Books Library Project will eventually achieve its goal of digitizing every book in the world, thereby diminishing the printed book, a medium that has lasted at least 3,000 years. Right now, the project looks impossible to complete, but with exponential change, years can easily become months, and months can easily become hours. We witnessed a similar phenomenon when scientist Craig Venter, PhD, and the United States government raced to create the first complete human genome. Thanks to advances in technology and analysis techniques, the project was completed ahead of schedule, with most of the progress made in the final two years once the work could reach a spectacular pace.

I believe Google's digitization project will greatly help libraries and will bring back thousands of out-of-print books, creating universal access that will ultimately benefit authors and readers alike. While some informational formats do disappear, some have staying power. The book will remain a viable tool in the future if we allow it to take on enhanced features offered through digital technology. We are not too far from the day when we can access every book on the planet through a comprehensive network of online libraries and a unified search engine. Other items and formats held in libraries, museums, and art galleries will become part of this network as well. As this digitization becomes more complete, the role of physical libraries will have to change to allow them to move from a focus on access to one of personalized learning and innovative content creation.

As libraries build their collections, they acquire a variety of successful formats, including print and digital materials. Today, most modern libraries have adopted an amazing array of digital technology, including high-speed Wi-Fi Internet as well as electronic journals, books, magazines, and newspapers, and a host of other emerging advancements.

I anticipate tomorrow's libraries offering enhanced e-books with universal access as well as embedded video and audio, among other features. And at some point, virtual reality simulations, artificial intelligence search engines, media content production equipment, and all sorts of innovations such as avatars and robotic assistants will no doubt become commonplace. (Before you set this book down and say, "Rubbish, it will never happen," feel free to skip ahead to Chapter 9 on Cool Tools and see that it is already happening.) The future is coming at us so quickly that many of us fail to realize that a lot of our ideas are already part of the past.

What's more, I believe the Internet will most likely change as well. It may break into more specialized versions, depending upon the marketplace's information needs, but it will most certainly evolve into a virtual environment offering far more tools than we have today.

STAY CALM AND CARRY ON

In 1984, futurist Alvin Toffler predicted in his book, *The Third Wave*, that we would move beyond one-size-fits-all standardization and a world where personalized products, jobs, and settings are possible. Certainly, this type of future could very well accommodate a variety of library designs, each customized to meet a unique community's needs.

Libraries could go in many different directions, and in this librarian's opinion, this kind of diversity is a good thing. My aim here is not to predict the future, but, instead, to provide you with the tools and concepts to create it. In the words of President Abraham Lincoln, "The best way to predict your future is to create it." Designer and inventor Buckminster Fuller later adapted Lincoln when he said, "The best way to predict the future is to design it." I think they were on to something.

These "library hybrids" will provide us with the resources we need to create content as well as the tools to access and analyze existing content. This isn't to say the traditional library, with its high bookshelves, giant ceilings, and grand chambers featuring secluded corners for deep reflective thought, will never be an option for communities wanting that type of setting; however, the idea of designing libraries to fit patrons' needs has always been a guiding principle of the ALA, and it's a practice I believe we need to continue.

I will present you the framework for one approach for transforming a library, but there is certainly room for many different perspectives on how to handle information literacy, curation, content creation, and cultural innovation.

DON'T FORGET YOUR MAP AND COMPASS

As any good scout or explorer will tell you, before you embark upon a journey into parts unknown, be sure you have your map and compass—or better yet, access to a GPS device. Knowing the lay of the land, where you are, and where you plan to go are always immensely helpful on life's journeys. History tells us where we have come from and where we have been. History also reminds us of where we have not been and possibly where we need to go, not to mention, where we are better off not going. I hope this chapter serves as a rough compass to guide us in a fruitful direction so we don't lose our way.

Before becoming a librarian, I worked as a school counselor for many years and trained as a school psychologist. During this time, I was strongly influenced by the work of Dr. Howard Gardner and his colleagues at Harvard University. Gardner's theory of multiple intelligences made complete sense when dealing with the diverse populations we find within our schools. The theory explains how one student may be terrible at math yet gifted in art, another may be a talented musician, yet less able in writing or verbal skills. The multiple intelligences theory and research behind it have become the scaffold for developing learning design studios and workspaces in our library. As you will read later, it is not the only map available for library transformation, but is the blueprint that guided my work.

Shortly after I started working on this book, I came across what has now become my favorite book about libraries: *The Atlas of New Librarianship*, written by David Lankes, PhD, a professor at and the director of the School of Information Studies of Syracuse University. Lankes' Atlas has provided me with an excellent theoretical basis for the work my colleagues and I have been doing at our library in Singapore.

While Gardner's and Lankes' work have provided me with maps, a lecture delivered by author Neil Gaiman titled "Why Our Future Depends on Libraries, Reading and Daydreaming" is an excellent compass. In his 2013 address to the Reading Agency, Gaiman said,

> *The simplest way to make sure that we raise literate children is to teach them to read, and to show them that reading is a pleasurable activity. And that means, at its simplest, finding books*

that they enjoy, giving them access to those books, and letting them read them.

He defends the value of fiction when he says:

You get to feel things, visit places and worlds you would never otherwise know. You learn that everyone else out there is a me, as well. You're being someone else, and when you return to your own world, you're going to be slightly changed.

Empathy is a tool for building people into groups, for allowing us to function as more than self-obsessed individuals.

You're also finding out something as you read that will be vitally important for making your way in the world. And it's this: THE WORLD DOESN'T HAVE TO BE LIKE THIS. THINGS CAN BE DIFFERENT.

Good libraries and good librarians encourage and support reading, and we support the kind of escapism Gaiman discusses in his article. After all, reading is our mainstay, our meat and potatoes, or for vegetarians, our healthy diet of culture. A good library offers both learning spaces devoted to readers who need quiet opportunities to reflect as well as more active spaces for discussions about books and ideas and for creation and innovation.

As you read through this book, you may at times wonder if I'm arguing for or against books or for or against quiet, reflective spaces. The truth is, I advocate for maker spaces, learning design studios, and emerging technologies, for new learning options designed for a variety of readers, researchers, projects, activities, subjects, learners, and learning styles. For me, it's never a question of either-or.

Traditional libraries offering comfort, quiet, and access to good books and literature are valuable assets, but these features may not be enough. Instead, we have to offer more to justify the substantial investment of time, money, and architecture required to create and maintain libraries. School libraries, especially, must offer resources, tools, and opportunities students cannot find in their classroom. In short, for libraries to survive, we must bravely and actively face the onslaught of exponential informational growth, unprecedented change, globalization, digitization, and social challenges unlike any we've ever witnessed in the history of mankind.

One last thought before I move on: while adapting to the demands of exponential change, we must be sure not to throw out time-honored values such as providing information on both sides of an issue, protecting our members' privacy, curating the best informational sources to save the reader and researcher time, and providing personalized service as learning coaches and informational mentors.

BUILD YOUR OWN LIBRARY

Several platforms allow you to create your own personal library cataloging system. Two of the most popular are GoodReads (Goodreads.com) and LibraryThing (librarything.com).

 TOOLKIT FOR RESEARCH ON LIBRARIES

See page 254 for links.

Association of College & Research Libraries (ACRL)
Libraries.org (United States only)
OCLC's Global Library Statistics
Pew Research Center
The Universal Digital Library (provides access to 1 million books)
US Institute of Museum and Library Services

CHAPTER 2

A Perfect Storm

Our intuition about the future is linear. But the reality of information technology is exponential, and that makes a profound difference. If I take thirty steps linearly, I get to thirty. If I take thirty steps exponentially, I get to a billion.

—Ray Kurzweil

Climate change is a hot topic these days, but it's not only the weather that's changing—technological advancements are also dramatically shifting the world's cultures and institutions. Digitization, globalization, the growth of social media, a knowledge explosion, and the very convergence of these driving forces are creating a rapid acceleration of change across all disciplines and all subject areas.

Every sector of society is experiencing these effects; however, I'm most concerned about the threat to education and libraries, which, I believe, is about to reach a "perfect storm."

The Great Wave off Kanagawa by Katsushika Hokusai

Bookstores are closing at a rapid rate, library budgets are being cut, and librarians are increasingly being asked to provide new services. The libraries that can adapt to their communities' demands for change will survive (and probably thrive), while those that resist will most likely become extinct.

BUDDY, CAN YOU SPARE A DIME?

In his article "The Ten Awful Truths about Book Publishing," Berrett-Koehler Publishers president Steven Piersanti noted that U.S. publishing industry sales peaked in 2007 and have either fallen or been flat in subsequent years, according to reports of the Association of American Publishers. Now, as a first-time author, this is all pretty depressing, especially since I was hoping to become a bazillionaire in at least one year's time.

How am I supposed to get rich when only a handful of librarians buy a single copy for their libraries? To paint an even grimmer picture,

Piersanti goes on to say, "A book has far less than a [1 percent] chance of being stocked in an average bookstore." I guess I need to cancel my exotic summer vacation…

Baby Boomers and Baby Busters

Among the many trends at work during these turbulent times are people living and working longer, which has profound consequences for public libraries which serve all age groups. The needs of library users are changing dramatically, especially from one generation to the next. School libraries have to adapt and respond to the heavy influence of social media with generation Z and deal with issues of fake news and unreliable sources.

Back to the Future

It's been said the sixties actually happened in the seventies. Case in point: In the seventies, women made significant gains toward equal rights, concern for the environment was at its highest level ever, the Civil Rights movement was taking hold, and the War on Poverty was in full swing. We were creating the future, or at least we thought we were. And then we dropped the ball. "Feminism" became a dirty word, economic growth became more important than protecting the environment, and poverty was left to be solved by market forces. In a way, we lost almost four decades' worth of social development, and only now are we taking another look at these key social issues. The point is, technological change builds on itself in a steady progression which is now turning into an exponential progression, while social change moves much more slowly and sometimes even reverses itself. Libraries have to deal with incredible technological change while adjusting to dramatic and uncertain social changes happening in our society.

Toffler believed the gap between the producer and the consumer would eventually fuse together to create a "prosumer," someone who could fill their own needs. Prosumer has now come to mean a person who both consumes and produces media. As I see it, the library patrons of tomorrow will essentially be prosumers—both consumers and producers of knowledge.

Four important forces are helping drive social and technological change: digitization, globalization, an information explosion, and the converging of all three, thereby creating exponential acceleration. Libraries are just one of many social institutions being affected by these forces. The thing is, though, libraries can offer other institutions the critical support they need to adapt to change.

FROM BITS AND BYTES TO EXABYTES

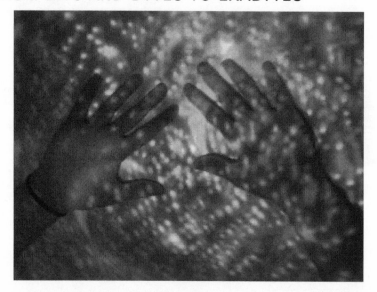

An Australian teenager created this photo titled "1st Time Delving into the Digital World." I think it nicely illustrates our immersion into a new digital space.

Source: Lydia Heise Flickr

All of the world's information is in the process of going digital, allowing us to easily share, duplicate, remix, and analyze it on more fronts than ever before. As a result of this increasing digitization, the Internet is rapidly becoming a kind of "world brain" that controls the key features of society, institutions, and technical networks. I would go so far as to say eventually the Internet of things will even be placing us in human-to-machine interactions unlike any we've never imagined. With virtual reality and augmented reality, we are beginning to merge our physical and digital worlds in ways that are hard to imagine.

In the case of libraries, doomsayers have been pointing to the digitization of books and information as the deathblow for libraries. I disagree. As librarians, we can (and must) embrace the digital era while also safeguarding our institutions against digitization's negative effects such as intrusions on personal privacy.

In "The Top Six Library Issues," journalist David Rothman warns, "Librarians, beware. Solo, patrons like me are no menace to America's public libraries. En masse, however, we could eventually kill off many libraries without even trying. Like a growing number of others, I favor e-books over paper books." Libraries are, of course, rapidly adopting e-books, but Rothman's assumption is that our places of work simply exist to offer library goers access, which is reflective of the current worldview. This must change. Libraries must move toward supporting cultural change through content creation. Those libraries offering only access to information will most likely perish, while libraries offering members the opportunity to build, create, problem solve, collaborate, network, innovate, and learn lifelong skills will become innovation hubs and critical social institutions that carry us through times of turbulent change.

Globalization was a major theme in *New York Times's* columnist Thomas Friedman's best-selling book *The World Is Flat*. In it, he shows how ten "flatteners," ranging from the end of the Cold War to the Internet and outsourcing, have created a more level playing field for the world's population. Globalization links culture, commerce, research, and innovation without the time-delay location once created.

In *The Race to the Top: The Real Story of Globalization*, Swedish journalist Thomas Larsson says globalization "is the process of world shrinkage, of distances getting shorter, things moving closer. It pertains to the increasing ease with which somebody on one side of the world can interact, to mutual benefit, with somebody on the other side of the world." Libraries must connect globally to be effective resources in today's world. Libraries cannot ignore large global social issues that impinge on our culture; they have a responsibility to help us think globally and to act locally.

"Information explosion" is an inadequate description of the situation we are entering—it's more like the Big Bang. In his 1982 book, Critical Path, philosopher Buckminster Fuller says that until 1900, human knowledge doubled approximately every century, and by the end of World War II, knowledge was doubling every twenty-five years. Today, things are not as simple, as different types of knowledge have different growth rates. For example, nanotechnology knowledge is doubling every two years and clinical knowledge every eighteen months. But on average, human knowledge is doubling every thirteen months. According to an IBM article titled "The Toxic Terabyte," the build-out of the Internet will lead to the world's information base "doubling in size every eleven hours." When speaking at the Techonomy conference in 2010, former Google CEO Eric Schmidt said there were five exabytes of information created between the dawn of civilization through 2003, but that much information is now created every two days—and the pace is increasing. Schmidt told his audience that he believes "the world is not ready for the technology revolution that will be happening to them soon."

In my personal view, librarians have a responsibility to help guide their patrons through this informational glut. We have to find more effective ways to separate the signal from the noise. Librarians are needed now more than ever to serve as curators of information helping us to find the best and most reliable sources.

ACCELERATION: SCREAM IF YOU WANT TO GO FASTER

The speed of social change   *Source: Eric E. Castro, Wikimedia Commons*

The speed of technological change   *Source: NASA, Wikimedia Commons*

The rate of change is dramatically accelerating as these forces converge with one another. In *The Singularity Is Near*, author Ray Kurzweil illustrates how informational change is taking us from linear change to exponential change. Our education system cannot keep pace using its current methods of teaching, and even the best core curriculum can only offer a general outline of the informational landscape. Libraries in turn cannot hope to have physical collections that even scratch the surface of this vast ocean of information. Digital resources will become more and more necessary and a greater degree of artificial intelligence will be utilized in our search engines. Librarians will continue to be the human interfaces for patrons baffled by technology, but they will also become problem solvers and facilitators for additional content creation. Technology has become so ubiquitous in our culture that we are faced with outdated social systems dealing with situations we have never faced. Even the most fundamental institutions, including schools, hospitals, and libraries, will have to quickly adapt or risk becoming dysfunctional, or even obsolete. We must devote an equal amount of time learning lifelong skills as we apply them to knowledge acquisition. Running faster and trying to learn everything is no longer a solution. We are entering an age where machines and artificial intelligence will challenge the human mind for supremacy. Science-fiction writer Isaac Asimov put forth his three laws of robotics in his novel *I, Robot*:

1. A robot may not injure a human being or, through inaction, allow a human being to come to harm.
2. A robot must obey orders given it by human beings except where such orders would conflict with the First Law.
3. A robot must protect its own existence as long as such protection does not conflict with the First or Second Law.

It is critical that we carefully consider the kinds of ethical systems we need to build into our technology as we move forward.

We, as librarians, will play an important role in this future: we will be the people to offer educators connections and opportunities for both collaboration and problem solving. Now, we may need to reintroduce them to philosophers' works and help with their research so they can clarify their values, solve the problems at hand, and better understand the consequences of the future we are building, but that is all certainly doable.

We will need to create learning spaces with resources and serve as facilitators to support, and even ignite, learning. We will be far more effective change agents in education than districtwide initiatives since we can offer teachers and students support for new types of learning without forcing it upon them. Unlike teachers, we have the freedom to go beyond the curriculum, to be more agile and experimental. The library is the perfect setting to test out new ideas, new technologies, and new ways to individualize and personalize education.

Who Cares?

Perhaps the greatest threat to libraries is apathy. Joe Average may very well say, "Who cares if libraries become extinct? I haven't stepped inside one for years, so does it really matter?" As librarians, we must provide value along with our library's services, spaces, equipment, and opportunities for patrons to create. Our profession needs a comprehensive plan, or better yet, several plans, to select from. Today, libraries only receive a patchwork of suggestions from the ALA and our professional journals, ranging from integrating maker spaces to community commons, without ever receiving a clear, overall strategy.

Librarians need to reach out and connect with patrons to understand their needs and show them our relevance. School librarians have a special responsibility in this regard; if students are exposed to old-fashioned libraries in schools, it is likely they will give up on academic and public libraries later in life. Rather being hit by the tsunami, we can use the forces of digitization, globalization, social media, and the explosion of information to harness the power and surf the wave of change.

CHAPTER 3

Everything Is a Remix, Even This Title

All ideas are secondhand, consciously and unconsciously drawn from a million outside sources. We are constantly littering our literature with disconnected sentences borrowed from books at some unremembered time and now imagined to be our own.

—*Mark Twain*

Much of what I propose in this book is a remix of ideas I've heard from many different quarters at many different times. As my University of Oregon advisor, psychologist Raymond Lowe, PhD, often said, "I have never had an original idea. Every time I think I have discovered something new, I find out someone else already thought of it." Lowe was an important leader in Adlerian psychology, and even though he may not have realized it, he did actually have many original ideas, among them the "remix factor."

Filmmaker Kirby Ferguson, who created the "Everything Is a Remix" video series, defines remix as the ability "to combine or edit existing materials to produce something new." And in his May 2016 video, "Everything's a Remix: The Force Awakens," he explains that, "For as long as humans have been creating, we have been copying, transforming, and combining." He continues to say, "Rather than simply copying, legal remix is often creative, additive, and enhancing." Ferguson respects the need for copyright laws to protect the rights of original creators but implies that these laws need to be revised to allow greater freedom of expression for those who build on that work.

As I mentioned earlier, Newton famously said, "If I have seen further than others, it is by standing on the shoulders of giants." In this same video, Ferguson contends Newton was doing just that when he adapted and remixed Bernard de Chartres' original twelfth-century quote which read, "We are like dwarfs on the shoulders of giants…"

Recently, my colleagues and I observed a group of young students working in SAS Elementary School's maker space. As we watched them, we were inspired and thought of new ideas for our own middle school studios. And then it hit me: the staff and I had come full circle— we were standing on the shoulders of children (dwarfs), which allowed us to see further into our own work.

I believe we now need to remix the concept of libraries by retaining the best elements of past and present libraries and then transforming and combining them with new elements from other fields and disciplines.

For example, let's take our original brand embodied in the Library of Alexandria and copy its best features. Now, let's transform those features and combine them with elements of modern technology and culture, as well as ideas from information science, psychology, and other fields. What results is a brand-new remix that promotes learning, entertainment, and social change.

Ferguson's video "Everything's a Remix: The Force Awakens" nicely illustrates the beauty of finding the perfect mix of the familiar and the new by copying, transforming, and combining, starting with the familiar and moving toward the novel.

FAMILIAR ⟶ SWEET SPOT ⟵ NOVEL

Though Ferguson doesn't use the term "sweet spot," he puts it more elegantly in his video, saying, "If you can create that perfect hybrid of the new and the old, the results can be explosive."

Today, the boundaries between copying, transforming, and combining are gray at best, reflecting the complex Byzantine nature of our copyright laws. Copyright laws are desperately in need of change and revision. Librarians no longer can count on the protections of Fair Use. European Union copyright laws often vary from American laws, and copyright lawyers can no longer predict how judges and courts will interpret the laws when faced with complex decisions that involve new technologies and rapid exchanges of information.

WALK LIKE AN EGYPTIAN

Let's look at the most highly regarded library ever created: the Library of Alexandria. Largely considered the ancient world's largest, most important, and most successful library, this third-century BCE institution attempted to collect the world's knowledge in one place. The Egyptian empire's scribes boarded each ship passing through the port of Alexandria, each tasked with hand copying all of the documents on board; these documents were then added to the collection at the Royal Library of Alexandria.

However, the Library of Alexandria was not simply a warehouse; rather, it served a much broader role in research, education, and culture than we often associate with libraries today, even featuring specialized rooms for astronomy and zoology, like a university.

Author Kelly Trumble points out in her book *The Library of Alexandria*, that this famous structure was the meeting place for the

The Great Library of Alexandria   *Source: Von Corven, Wikimedia Commons*

New Library of Alexandria   *Source: Carsten Whimster, Wikimedia Commons*

era's great minds including Euclid, Archimedes, Hypatia and many others. The royal family invited visiting scholars to speak at gatherings and welcomed them and their families for extended stays and collaboration, much like the modern-day sabbaticals university professors take. As my colleague Doug Tindall once said to me, "In a sense, the Library of Alexandria created the first TED Talks."

Thus, it is part of the ancient tradition of libraries to be more than mere book depositories, which is why I propose a remix of the Alexandria model. By adding features such as learning design studios, a center for emerging technologies, and specialized zones for content creation and knowledge facilitation, we can catch up with our past while advancing more dynamic roles and functions. Our remixed libraries should allow members to freely interact, share creation tools, and innovate in agile and flexible spaces. If we want to meet the demands of the Digital Age, we must adapt—and adapt quickly.

THE LIBRARY OF THE FUTURE'S ROLE

Schools are facing enormous challenges in the twenty-first century, and more than ever, educators need our support to meet these challenges head-on. It's tempting to look at school libraries and wonder if we can afford these large physical structures that could easily become dinosaurs in the Information Age. The services within school libraries can be adapted to move beyond the traditional school curriculum and support all forms of learning, including project- and inquiry-based exploration. The library of the future must become a supportive hub where students can problem solve, create, and understand the world in new ways. Librarians must collaborate with teachers to assist students in gaining a thorough understanding of information literacy, as outlined by the ALA's *Standards for the 21st-Century Learner*, but they must move beyond research and access into content creation, anything less, and we may not be able to justify the library's existence.

CHAPTER 4

That's So Yesterday

We look at the present through a rear view mirror. We march backwards into the future.

—Marshall McLuhan

I have visited many academic, school, and public libraries and have talked to many librarians, and I've noticed that we all seem to be looking for answers about how to forge ahead. The ALA is a venerable institution with dedicated and talented individuals supporting libraries in numerous ways, but it isn't providing librarians with clear direction for sailing into this perfect storm. In 1998, the ALA published *Information Power*, a handy guide for librarians. The guide was later replaced with the much briefer and less descriptive *Standards for the 21st-Century Learner*. The new standards sounded good, but they were so broad that it has been difficult for librarians to understand what specific actions need to be taken. How are librarians supposed to integrate information literacy into the school curriculum while also redesigning our libraries to facilitate creation content?

Libraries must respond to their communities' needs, and because of that, there is no one perfect library model, nor will there ever be. But it's difficult to point to a single library, albeit public, academic, or school, willing to take risks and provide a framework to explore, all the while showing the rest of us the way, like a lighthouse. That's why I wrote this book: my colleagues and I haven't solved the riddle or cut the Gordian knot, but we have tried new approaches, some of which have been quite effective. If you read the numerous books, blogs, websites, and articles discussing the libraries of the future, they usually highlight one or two features, such as introducing a maker space or using new technology to highlight learning. Together, it all seems a bit of a hodgepodge, with an idea here and there, but without a single coherent plan or framework.

Unfortunately, we can't turn to schools of library and information science, which are dominated by theorists. As in most cases, it is far more challenging to put theory into practice when faced with time, budget, and political constraints, and that's not to mention the diverse range of facilities, backgrounds, and skill levels each of us encounter daily in our settings. The only way to really understand the needs of a school librarian is to work with hundreds of children of diverse ages and backgrounds, day in and day out.

The fields of psychology and education have moved from behaviorism to cognitivism to constructivism to social constructivism and some experimentation with connectivism. These theoretical frameworks have all influenced our educational practice and the work of school librarians. Today, when discussing twenty-first-century education, most people are referring to educational practices largely based on constructivist thought. The sixties and seventies saw a brand of alternative education known as "progressivism," which looked something like constructivism. We left progressivism behind, and psychologists slammed the door on right-brain models until neurology forced the issue back into view four decades later. Education has a tendency to move in spirals—we come full circle every decade or so as companies selling new curriculum unveil models using new buzzwords, capturing old ideas in new ways.

In 1977, I was a student teacher at Sam Barlow High School in Gresham, Oregon, and was amazed by the work done as part of a highly innovative and successful program called "Project Viewpoint." The educators' approach focused on highlighting the right brain's skills to balance education's preoccupation with left-brain functions and included work with metaphors, music, art, visualization, and hands-on learning. (Daniel Pink's book *A Whole New Mind* echoes many of this era's thoughts.)

Libraries have been largely untouched by all of this chatter, instead opting to continue providing access to resources and information, with information literacy seen as the "great advance forward." Excuse me if I'm cynical, but in the past few decades, libraries have seemingly functioned much like workhorses pulling heavy wagons while wearing blinders. When I entered the profession in 1996, flagship institutions like the University of Chicago and Columbia University had abandoned their library science programs and the profession appeared in trouble—but libraries were seen as too big to fail. During the last twenty years, libraries have been slow in responding to the forces of change, yet school libraries are in the perfect position to serve as catalysts for educational change. In most schools, the library has a large physical footprint, controls a larger-than-average budget, and provides a neutral testing ground for curricular changes. Rather than waiting to be told what to do, librarians must become leaders and agents of change. We can try new programs and new approaches without having to change the whole educational system. We can also experiment with maker spaces and other innovative spaces and then invite our colleagues in to test out new ideas for learning.

FLIP YOUR LIBRARY

In "flipped classrooms," the teachers often create videos to demonstrate concepts to students at home, allowing students to pause the video, play it more than once, and move as quickly or slowly through the material as they need. This then frees the teacher to serve as a learning coach and more effectively address each student's individual learning needs. In short, a flipped classroom moves from the "sage on the stage" model of teaching to the "guide on the side" approach. Fortunately, librarians have always functioned more like a "guide on the side," so that's the easy part. However, flipping a library isn't quite the same as flipping a math class.

In the library's case, how students conduct research is turned on its head. For example, in a flipped library, students still come to the library to access books and other resources, but they also come to design projects, create systems, use materials, and gain understanding. To facilitate this kind of work, libraries must provide students with personalized learning environments to accommodate individual work, group work, specialized tech equipment, and just-in-time assistance from a variety of learning coaches. Although most libraries don't have these sorts of resources right now, we can begin moving in that direction. And since having staff available to meet all sorts of learning needs is very important but not always possible with limited budgets, the library can invite classes in and collaborate with teachers to serve as coaches to find solutions.

BUT WHY ARE YOU DOING THAT?

In his TED Talk titled "How Great Leaders Inspire Action," best-selling author Simon Sinek provides us with a simple, yet effective, insight to inspire action: he says most of us can easily explain what we do and how we do it, but we often lose sight of why we do it.

This question "Why?" represents our purpose, our cause, and our belief, which drives our passion. As Sinek says, "People don't buy what you do; they buy why you do it." If you have a passion for your work and you can explain why, people will be more likely to adopt your product or service. So, in the context of the library, if members understand why your library is set up the way it is and why you operate as a facilitator rather than the typical librarian or a teacher, then they will be far more likely to trust and identify with the services you're offering.

When my school's admissions officers take new families on tours, they always come into the library. Visitors are often surprised to see our library's Wellness Zone equipped with fitness equipment as well as the other learning studios and activities going on. What we do in these settings is fairly self-evident, but when we explain why we do these things, you can see the families' heads nodding and a deeper understanding taking hold. When my colleagues and I explain why we are engaged in facilitating so many ways of learning, we're helping our visitors understand and appreciate the added features our library offers. Explaining our library's why has been, and will continue to be, critical to our success.

Your Mission, If You Choose to Accept It

As you'll read in later chapters, the school library I work in emphasizes helping students facilitate their learning through the "eight signs of intelligence," a theory set forth by psychology professor Howard Gardner, PhD. His multiple intelligences theory along with Lankes' mission statement and theoretical work provide the "why" for what I am proposing. Reading is a powerful learning tool derived from verbal linguistic intelligence, but we also learn in many other ways including logical mathematical, kinesthetic, interpersonal, intrapersonal, visual-spatial, musical acoustics, and naturalistic intelligences.

> *The mission of librarians is to improve society through facilitating knowledge creation in their communities.*
> —*David Lankes,* The Atlas of New Librarianship

In our library, we see this "why" as going hand in hand with Lankes' mission statement for librarians, reminding us that we are there so we can help give our members a greater sense of clarity and purpose. And though his mission statement radically differs from almost every other mission statement I've been exposed to as a librarian, it perfectly fits the work we're doing in Singapore.

Lankes bases his approach, including his mission statement for librarians, on conversation theory, which focuses on learning and knowledge. "This is a departure from the current focus on information, access, and artifacts," Lankes explains the important role librarians can play in the learning process.

> *As a librarian, you value learning. This comes from our mission as learning is defined as the acquisition of knowledge. We feel that all sectors of our community, from prisoner to prince, deserve the opportunity to learn. We also value learning in all of its varied contexts, from quiet solitary contemplation, to online learning to informal investigations. The only thing that trumps the need to learn is the need to improve society.*

Here is the SAS Middle School Library's motto, mission, and vision. (As you can see, I have borrowed extensively from Lankes.)

Motto: Everything is connected.

Mission: To facilitate learning and knowledge creation. We will assist members in becoming thoughtful users and creators of information with an emphasis on improving society through lifelong learning.

Vision: To connect people and ideas; to connect the arts and the sciences; to connect literature with social concerns; and to connect learning with overall wellness and human development. Along the way, we want students to experience the pure joy that comes with discovering and creating new things to improve society.

TEN KEY PRINCIPLES

In 2009, professors Cathy Davidson and David Theo Goldberg wrote The Future of Learning Institutions in a Digital Age. In it, they discuss "ten principles for the future of learning," which I believe are relevant to libraries and educational institutions. This report, produced by John D. and Catherine T. MacArthur Foundation, addresses the need for interdisciplinary collaboration in dealing with the forces of digital change. I had the opportunity to meet with Cathy Davidson in 2012 and briefly discussed the implications this report holds for libraries and other learning institutions.

The ten principles advocated in the report are:

1. **Self-Learning**: Empower individuals to become independent learners.
2. **Horizontal Structures**: No longer abide by the belief that top-down hierarchies are the most effective ways to structure learning.
3. **From Presumed Authority to Collective Credibility**: Respect and use the work of highly effective groups of dedicated amateurs as well as established experts in the field.
4. **A De-Centered Pedagogy**: Apply crowdsourcing approaches to learning using social media models, such as Wikipedia.
5. **Networked Learning**: Participate in collaborative learning through physical and social networks while using this as an avenue for individualized learning.

6. **Open Source Education**: Trust in a culture that promotes knowledge building as a collaborative effort developed through conversations with many sources.
7. **Learning as Connectivity and Interactivity**: Use social networks and mobile devices to connect individuals and promote new forms of collaborative interaction.
8. **Lifelong Learning**: Adapt to novel situations in an increasingly complex world by constantly learning skills and knowledge.
9. **Learning Institutions as Mobilizing Networks**: Create flexible and agile environments to provide accidental collisions between disciplines and types of people.
10. **Flexible Scalability and Simulation**: Adopt new learning models to keep up with the incredible acceleration of change.

THE TORTOISE AND THE HARE

Libraries transformed into library innovation centers are perfect settings for implementing Davidson and Goldberg's ten principles for the future of learning. Adapting to exponential growth in knowledge isn't simply a matter of running faster or working harder—we'll never keep up. Instead, it's a matter of working smarter.

We must move as quickly as we can toward higher-order skills, including problem solving, critical thinking, analysis, synthesis, and information literacy and move away from trying to cover each subject's content in its entirety.

I realize social change moves far more slowly than technology, and that school cultures are among the most resistant to change. And time and time again, we see culture winning out over strategy. But, if we try, our libraries can become innovation centers, where teachers and students try new approaches to learning and receive professional support in the process. As a result, we may begin adopting new roles as "learning design specialists," successfully bridging the gap between technology, information, and learners. The ten principles from HASTAC will help guide our work in libraries and schools by promoting self-learning, horizontal learning structures, connectivity, and lifelong learning.

ELEVATOR SPEECH

Schools, communities, and libraries are actively searching for ways to keep pace with our rapidly changing digital world. The environment, health, economic inequality, poverty, immigration, and other global problems and concerns cut across political and geographical boundaries. As the old saying goes, we need to think globally and act locally. We need to leverage our expanding knowledge base and emerging technologies and transform our libraries into service learning centers fostering innovation and knowledge creation. Combined, they can serve as catalysts for change within communities and schools.

I propose we experiment in our libraries, that we create mash-ups and hybrid settings based on our communities' needs and initiatives. While there is no one perfect model for the library of the future, there are a range of models available. School libraries can offer learning design studios and maker spaces for knowledge creation; academic libraries can conduct in-house, action-based research with students and faculty working together across disciplines; and public libraries can loan their resources and engage communities in designing spaces based on local needs. These types of libraries will all need staff members who are facilitators for knowledge creation and networkers for social change.

CHAPTER 5

Censored

What is freedom of expression? Without the freedom to offend, it ceases to exist.

—Salman Rushdie

Sorry, you are banned from reading this chapter.

Just kidding.

ALA ethical standards restrict librarians from releasing information on the circulation habits of individual patrons. It has always been a long-standing practice for librarians to maintain confidentiality of records regarding checkouts. Imagine if a student checked out a book on pregnancy and another student or adult wanted to know who had that book. Librarians have an obligation to keep that information private. The student may have the book checked out for research purposes, or she may be worried that she is pregnant. Whom she decides to share this information with is her business and is not the right of the librarian to disclose.

The digital age presents many new challenges and tensions in the way we balance our need for free access to information against personal privacy needs. Video cams, sensors, credit cards, GPS devices, and social media have made our lives far more open to inspection than ever before. Librarians have to protect the rights of individuals while upholding the rights of freedom of information.

Too often, well-meaning people with strong opinions about protecting children or safeguarding the public will take on the crusade of cleansing a library of work they regard as "smut"—you know, distasteful, wrong, offensive, pornographic, dangerous, or insulting. However, Article Three of the ALA's Library Bill of Rights very clearly states, "Libraries should challenge censorship in the fulfillment of their responsibility to provide information and enlightenment."

The ALA also says it recognizes that library patrons may challenge books or other materials because of concerns about the content's suitability. (See Figure 5.1, page 48.) In response, the organization writes on its "Challenge Support" page, "A challenge is an attempt to remove or restrict materials, based upon the objections of a person or group. Challenges do not simply involve a person expressing a point of view; rather, they are an attempt to remove material from the curriculum or library, thereby restricting the access of others."

Today, most libraries have book challenge procedures to handle requests to remove or restrict access to certain materials, but I've found it is always helpful to have a library advisory committee, upon which the librarian sits, to make judgments on these cases.

During my fifteen years of librarianship, I've only had a small number of challenges, and in most cases, they were memorable and tense, as there were usually strong convictions on both sides. My record year was 2007, when I had four challenges—more than in my entire career—covering almost all of our informational formats, including magazines, books, CDs, and videos. This is rare, but it shows how parental anxieties can build when one parent calls another and a movement begins.

In the first case, one staunchly conservative parent was furious that we subscribed to Maclean's, a Canadian magazine, because it had a photo of President George W. Bush wearing a beret with the caption, "How Bush Became the New Saddam."

The second involved Perry Moore's fiction novel, *Hero*, which depicts a boy who discovers he is gay and a superhero. The mother with the complaint was so mad she could hardly contain herself. When I asked her which content exactly she found offensive, she said, "Here, read this—these two boys are kissing!"

The third involved a video documentary about Egypt mentioning prostitution. In this case, the concerned party was actually a teacher worried about parents' reactions.

And the fourth case was a CD by singer Avril Lavigne with lyrics that a parent found offensive.

It was a challenging year (no pun intended), and with the ALA's librarian resources at my side to help guide me, I attempted the art of diplomacy as I worked through each situation. My goal was to explain to the parents and the teacher that the materials we judge appropriate help prepare their children for real-life challenges they may face by offering safe, early exposure and allowing them time to reflect on the situation at hand. Sensitive themes in books and other informational formats offer an opportunity for both parents and teachers to have conversations that would otherwise lack context.

If you ever encounter challenge cases such as these, my advice is to adopt a listening attitude and try not to be defensive. I know it's difficult when you are taking a phone call in the midst of dealing with a host of school problems or if you receive an email late at night written by an angry parent fueled by a bit too much alcohol. Before returning that call or replying to the email, do your homework and have some options in mind.

Although each case involves a long story, in short, the Maclean's issue arose on Friday and the next issue was due to take its place on the library's shelves Monday, so I informed the parent it would be replaced. We, however, continued our subscription to the magazine, as it had a long track record of excellent journalistic reviews. When the parent pursued the issue by asking, "Are all the magazines you subscribe to ultra-liberal like this one?" I replied, "Let me send you our magazine list and you decide for yourself. If you think we have a strong liberal bias, please recommend some good magazines that will work for our population." In the end, the parent felt heard and the conversation was polite and ended well. I never received any magazine suggestions.

In the second case, the parent loomed over my desk, refusing to have a chair, and insisted that I ban *Hero* before students were infected with ideas of homosexuality. I asked her if she had read the entire book and encouraged her to do so when she replied that she had enough information from the passage she found. She completed our challenge form (See Figure 5.2, page 49.), and after reading the book, our committee unanimously decided to keep it in the collection. Based on the committee discussions, I replied to the parent via email to explain the reasons for our decision, including the book's merits (of which there are many) and the stance our school takes in support of the ALA Freedom to Read provisions. I also explained that under our challenge guidelines, parents have the right to appeal the committee's decision.

The parent replied that she was very unhappy, but she did not apply for an appeal.

In the case of the video documentary challenge, we decided to add a note about the sensitive section to alert teachers that part of the film offered a rich opportunity to discuss an ancient social issue.

Finally, in the case of the CD, we decided to trade our CD to the high school for one that was more appropriate for our student population. This may seem like a cop-out, but in some cases, libraries, like the United States Supreme Court, may decide not to decide and wait for a more clear-cut case to make a stand on censorship.

A WORD OF ADVICE

Schools are notorious for having too many committees and too many meetings; nevertheless, it is helpful to solicit outsiders' input on library matters in the form of a library advisory committee. I suggest forming this committee by selecting three individuals whom you respect and trust and who are not afraid to offer honest criticism and helpful suggestions. In addition to offering advice on collection development and library services, the library advisory committee should be prepared to deliberate on book or materials challenges when needed. Once I've formed the committee, I usually spend one meeting going over the ALA's Library Bill of Rights and Code of Ethics as well as some of the other documents listed in "Toolkit" on the following page. Then, if a patron requests the removal of any library material, it is this committee that reviews the challenge and makes a decision. As the librarian, I simply write the committee's decision and pass it along to the school principal. (Maybe I should consider renaming our committee "Serious Matters in Understanding Text" or "SMUT" for short.)

The ALA offers this sample reconsideration procedure below:

RECONSIDERATION PROCEDURE

1. A patron challenging material should meet with the librarian to state objections and offer possible solutions. The librarian should explain the school's philosophy and goals and the library media center's selection policy in an attempt to resolve the challenge informally.

2. If the challenge is not resolved, the patron should complete the "Materials Challenge Form" and return it to the librarian.

3. The librarian will share the form and notes from the initial meeting with the principal.

4. The librarian will submit the challenge to a divisional library advisory committee, which will then review the material in question and recommend a solution.

5. The committee will provide a report to the principal that includes a professional recommendation about the material.

6. The principal's decision concerning the committee's recommendation will be sent in writing to the complainant with a copy to the superintendent. If the complaint is valid, the principal will acknowledge it and explain the recommended changes. If the item is to be retained, an explanation of the decision will be given.

7. If the complainant is still unsatisfied with the result of the investigation, they may appeal to the board of directors, who will then review the complaint and make a final decision that will stand under all circumstances.

Figure 5.1

Challenged Work

Title _____

Author or Editor _____

Copyright Date _____

Publisher _____

Type of Work _____

(e.g., book, play, e-book, video, audio, artwork, periodical, or etc.)

Initiator of Challenge

Name _____

Telephone _____

Email _____

Grounds for Challenge (Check all that apply.)

Cultural	Sexual	Values	Social Issues
__ Anti-Ethnic	__ LGBT	__ Anti-Family	__ Abortion
__ Insensitivity	__ Nudity	__ Offensive	__ Drugs
__ Racism	__ Sex Ed	Language	__ Occult
__ Other	__ Sexually Explicit	__ Drugs	__ Suicide
		__ Political View	
		__ Religious View	

Please answer the following questions after reading, viewing, or listening to the material in its entirety. If the space provided is not enough, attach additional sheets.

1. What do you object to in the material? (Please be specific, citing page numbers, place on the video, etc.)
2. What do you believe is the theme or purpose of this material?
3. What do you feel might be the result of a student using this material?
4. For what age group would you recommend this material?
5. What would you like the school to do about this material?

Do not assign or recommend it to my child _____

Other (please specify): _____

Figure 5.2

TOOLKIT OF RESOURCES FOR BOOK AND MATERIAL CHALLENGES

See page 257 for links.

- Challenge Support
- Challenged Materials
- Checklist and Ideas for Library Staff Working with Community Leaders
- Code of Ethics
- Core Values of Librarianship
- Developing a Confidentiality Policy
- Developing a Public Library Internet Use Policy
- Freedom to Read
- Freedom to View Statement
- Interpretations of the Library Bill of Rights
- Libraries: An American Value
- Library Bill of Rights

CHAPTER 6

Where's Wally?
(Accessing Info)

Toto, I've a feeling we're not in Kansas anymore.

—Dorothy, The Wizard of Oz

I t's time to address the elephant in the room: the Internet.
Helping our patrons access reliable information has always been librarians' primary goal, and as we make our way into the twenty-first century, it will remain an important part of our work. But the information landscape is rapidly changing, and when it comes to accessing information, nothing comes close to the Internet. Most people doing research today start (and often end) on the Internet, so it only makes sense for us to become experts in conducting online searches. (When I say "expert" in this case, I mean staying current on the search engines' latest features, as Google and its peers are continually updating their products.)

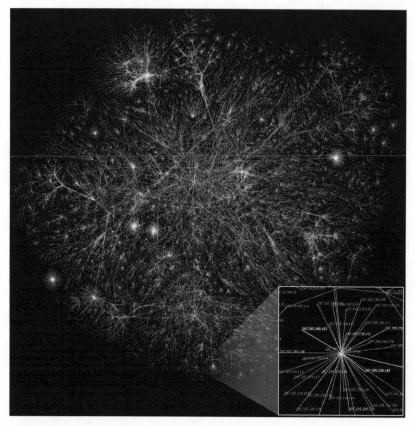

Partial Map of the Internet   *Source: The OPTE Project, Wikimedia Commons*

Current search engines only search a fraction of the information on the worldwide web. The accuracy and authenticity of information varies widely and the proliferation of fake news has become a growing problem. Librarians are faced with the task of trying to teach members advanced search skills in a constantly changing digital environment. In a sense, we are all newcomers operating in beta mode as we constantly adjust the manner in which we navigate the digital world and its countless sources of information.

Among our digital information sources are the huge book collections and other print formats continuing to go digital, offering us an amazing level of access to information. In the not-too-distant future,

I predict we'll be able to use our mobile devices to check out e-books from such extensive collections as the Library of Congress. And we may find many great works that quickly went out of print—including scholarly books and other manuscripts—return to life, thanks to the Google Books Library Project. Though it's nowhere near completion, the Library Project is already providing us with access to more printed materials than ever before. And although I am well aware of the debates and controversies surrounding this project, in the long run, I think this project will be a good thing for authors, publishers, and readers alike.

As library goers themselves produce an increasing amount of informational content, they'll need more support with content creation than accessing content. Libraries whose staffs strive to facilitate these needs will survive, but I highly doubt those simply offering access will remain open for the long haul. In my opinion, this is not an either-or situation—our libraries need to offer both convenient access to information and facilitate learning by helping members with content creation. A few ancient ones will most likely survive as access points for archival information, much like museums, but the vast majority of public, academic, and school libraries will need to offer increasingly more services to not only attract, but also retain, their members.

INFORMATION LITERACY

Just as there is a growing gap between the literate and the illiterate in our society, there is an equally large gap between the tech savvy and those people feeling frustrated and overwhelmed by technology. Luckily, librarians can support reading while also serving as a human interface between bewildered citizens and the complex web of information and technology before them. This is a challenging job, to be sure, but it is also an exciting, rewarding one.

Effectively accessing information requires query formulation; selecting effective search terms; targeting the search by date, domain, publisher, or other variables; and understanding how to evaluate sources and judge the credibility of the information obtained. Librarians can facilitate members' learning of these skills by holding "info lit" workshops and modeling good search habits. Of course, search engines will change over time, as will natural language processing and more sophisticated artificial intelligence tools, but, nevertheless, we can go a long way in facilitating members' understanding of basic search techniques using resources like Google Guide (bit.ly/2hZ4y7Z).

(Note: Google is used by more people than any other search engine; however, if the stock market has taught us anything, it is not wise to always follow the herd. Investigate specialized search engines on specific content. Check out *The Next Web's* picks for "30 Specialized Search Engines Focused on Specific Content" to test as alternatives (bit.ly/2hpVMzp).

AGE OF THE PAGE

As I began experimenting with search techniques, I was surprised by how difficult it can be to determine when a website was created or updated. Knowing the age of a page is essential in determining if the information on a website or article is accurate and up-to-date. Using Google search, I turned to webpages Google developed to find the most up-to-date tips. Even then, I was amazed to find that it's difficult to locate pages' time stamps. During my research, I found the following articles helpful in determining webpages' ages:

- "Finding the Age of a Page" (bit.ly/2hbbL8o)
- "How to Carbon-Date a Web Page" (bit.ly/2i8UZ9X)
- "How Do I Find out When a Web Page Was Written?" (bit.ly/2hSpaPK)

As you delve into the world of search engines, you'll notice some search features have been around for a long time, while others have come and gone. To stay current, researchers have to constantly keep testing the search engines' new features. The following sites and articles are useful for staying in the know about Google's algorithm changes and search engine optimization:

- Search Engine Watch (bit.ly/2ie3TPh)
- 9to5 Google (bit.ly/2h0Fiwz)
- HubSpot's "Tips & Tricks for Searching Google Like a Pro"
- Moz's "Google Algorithm Change History"
- Moz's "Keyword Explorer" (bit.ly/2i8Ugpg)
- Search Engine Land's "Google: Algorithm Updates"
- Search Engine Watch

THE DEEP WEB

I find it surprising that librarians rarely call attention to the full scope of the Internet, including not just the "surface web" but also the "deep web." When I say "surface web," I'm referring to the portion of the worldwide web readily accessed by the standard search engines we use on a daily basis. On the other hand, the "deep web," "invisible web," or "hidden web" includes everything standard search engine queries won't pull up, including government publications, web mail, corporate information, and private networks. Nevertheless, much of the deep web can be accessed using direct URLs.

A Wikipedia entry on the dark web states, "The dark web is the [worldwide web] content that exists on darknets which use the public Internet but which require specific software, configurations, or authorization to access. The dark web forms a small part of the deep web."

According to WorldWideWebSize.com, Google's Index of the surface web is close to 50 billion web pages. In contrast, "Some estimates have pegged the size of the deep web at up to 500 times larger." A 2001 paper titled "The Deep Web: Surfacing Hidden Value" from the Journal of Electronic Publishing estimated that the deep web consists of about 7.5 petabytes.

To put all of this in perspective, check out Figure 6.1 below.

HOW BIG IS A PETABYTE, EXABYTE, ZETTABYTE, OR A YOTTABYTE?

1 Kilobyte (KB) = 1,024 bytes — 2 KB = One typewritten page

1 Megabyte (MB) = 1,024 KB — 1 MB = A small novel

1 Gigabyte (GB) = 1,024 MB — 1 GB = A pickup truck filled with paper

1 Terabyte (TB) = 1,024 GB — 10 TB = The Library of Congress's print collection

1 Petabyte (PB) = 1,024 TB — 2 PB = All of the academic research libraries in the United States' combined print collections

1 Exabyte (EB) = 1,024 PB — 5 Exabytes = All the words ever spoken

1 Zettabyte (ZB) = 1, 000 EB — In 2009 the entire World Wide Web was estimated to contain close to 500 exabytes, which is approximately equal to one half zettabyte.

1 Yottabyte = 1000 ZB

Figure 6.1   *Source: High Scalability Blog*

Many librarians are already super searchers and are well aware of the challenges posed in seeking out the best sources of digital information. Information literacy skills must become a larger feature in our school curriculum, and librarians have an obligation to keep up-to-date on the best methods for accessing and evaluating information sources.

THE MANY FORMS OF LITERACY

If we ever hope to function in this world and understand what's going on around us, we must possess literacy skills. "Information literacy" is a broad term encompassing skills in locating, using, synthesizing, evaluating, and communicating all sorts of information. There are several established models for teaching information literacy, including the Big Six model (big6.com/) developed by Mike Eisenberg, PhD, and the Web Quest model (webquest.org) developed by Bernie Dodge, PhD. In addition, NoodleTools and the SCONUL Seven Pillars of Information Literacy 9 (bit.ly/2i9qFMw) are very useful resources.

Many types of literacies have been identified, but there is no clear consensus on what actually constitutes a literacy. Antero Garcia provided this list in a blog post titled "The Many Forms of Literacy":

- **Digital**: Cognitive skills used in executing tasks in digital environments

- **Computer**: Using a computer and software

- **Media**: Thinking critically about different types of media

- **Information**: Evaluating, locating, identifying, and effectively using information

- **Technology**: Effectively using technology in a myriad of ways

- **Political**: Possessing the knowledge and skills needed to actively participate in political matters

- **Cultural**: Understanding one's culture

- **Multicultural**: Knowing and appreciating other cultures

- **Visual Literacy**: Critically analyzing images

Source: DIGITAL IS by Antero Garcia (bit.ly/2hTJnqI)

Okay, I realize this is all a bit overwhelming and beyond the time and scope we librarians alone can handle. School leaders and teachers need to explore and integrate many, if not all, of these forms of literacy into their curricula, rather than presenting them as standalone modules. Having said that, I know many school librarians who have learned through firsthand experience that trying to get schools to integrate information literacy at the very least is difficult. That's why sometimes we must take the lead and create the time, place, and curriculum for teaching information literacy basics. However, if standalone modules are the agreed-upon option, it's essential that they tie into the current curriculum to ensure students can apply the concepts to their work.

CURATION NATION

Who has time to sift through all the world's information? No one, of course, has that kind of time, not even full-time collection development specialists. There is simply too much information for one curator to handle. But with an army of curators and sophisticated technology tools, we can do a decent job of separating the wheat from the chaff.

As librarians, it is our job to help our colleagues and libraries' patrons identify essential information and then access and evaluate the best sources. With social media increasingly taking the place of traditional books and journalism, there is an ever-increasing need for curation and evaluation of our information sources.

CHAPTER 7

The New Creationism

Our libraries should transition to places to do stuff, not simply places to get stuff. The library will become a laboratory in which community members tinker, build, learn, and communicate. We need to stop being the grocery store or candy store and become the kitchen.

—*Joan Frye Williams*

Think of the transition from strictly offering access to content to now creating content as being on a continuum, with access supporting creation. As librarians, we will always play an important role in supporting our patrons' information literacy needs and curating the best sources of information for them, but we have to offer much more than this to remain viable.

As is true of most great ideas, the idea of libraries' services being on a continuum isn't new; in fact, it dates as far back as 1999, when Belmont Abbey College director of library services Donald Beagle wrote about "a new model for service delivery in academic libraries [that could] offer 'a continuum of service' from information retrieval to original knowledge creation." (Talk about a slow train coming—it's been almost twenty years since Beagle wrote those words!)

Excuse the pun, but perhaps the Beagle has landed.

THE GENESIS OF CREATION

When I tell friends about the maker space movement in schools, the typical response is, "We did that when I was a kid!" Why did schools get rid of all those great wood shops, metal shops, and other maker space areas? Simply put, because hands-on education has always taken a back seat to academic training.

While plumbers and electricians are obviously valuable members of our society, they've been assigned a lower status than, say, lawyers and bankers. Philosopher and mechanic Matthew Crawford writes in *Shop Class as Soulcraft*:

> It was in the 1990s that shop class started to become a thing of the past, as educators prepared students to become "knowledge workers." The disappearance of tools from our common education is the first step toward a wider ignorance of the world of artifacts we inhabit. And, in fact, an engineering culture has developed in recent years in which the object is to "hide the works," rendering many of the devices we depend on every day unintelligible to direct inspection.

Fortunately, this trend is finally changing, as educators are rediscovering the intrinsic value of engaging students in inquiry- and project-based learning, which often involves hands-on work. And thanks to books like Daniel Pink's *A Whole New Mind*, the educational community is beginning to view hands-on learning as a mixture of critical thinking, problem solving, creativity, and collaboration, rather than simply manual labor.

But to access these higher-level thinking skills, we need maker spaces and design centers, places where students have the freedom to experiment with design, building, and construction and find a balance between digital and analog solutions. We need places where students can try and even invent tools, approaches, and solutions to the problems before them.

There are very few areas within today's schools where project-based learning can take place. You need open space, proper tools, building materials, and safety procedures to support maker spaces, design centers, and tinkering corners. And while I'm not proposing that we convert all of our libraries into wood shops, I am suggesting that libraries can support the establishment of learning spaces to facilitate knowledge creation.

As we design our maker spaces, one of the key questions will be: Should we narrowly frame them to simply involve the creation of physical products? Or should we broaden them to include media production, such as musical compositions, digital art, or videos?

Today's students are increasingly turning to YouTube to show what they're learning about history, science, math, and other subjects in the form of compelling presentations. So as you consider adding media studios to your library's range of services, you must also think about how you'll instruct our students to care for and use the equipment as well as if you'll limit its use to within the library, a decision that will largely depend on how many devices you have and whether or not you're prepared to deal with potential loss and repair issues.

While this may all initially sound rather daunting, I encourage you to start by focusing on the areas most relevant to your community's needs and handle only as much as your staffing and budgets permit. As you begin setting up your video studio, I highly recommend not purchasing high-end video equipment—in most cases, an inexpensive, easy-to-use smartphone or tablet can easily meet members' video production needs. In fact, you could simply have a single iPad and one wall painted green. Once you see how users respond to your setup, you can go from there.

LENDING TOOLS

Typically, public libraries have been among the first to experiment with sharing physical tools with its members. As far back as 1976, the city of Columbus, Ohio, opened The RTCO Tool Library, lending tools to repair and upgrade homes. In 1978 and 1979, respectively, the Phinney Neighborhood Association Tool Lending Library and the Berkeley Public Library's Tool Library were established. All three still exist today.

Though they're still rather rare in the library world, recently, more and more tool libraries have opened in America and Canada, as well as several other countries. This may become the new norm, as libraries begin focusing on facilitating knowledge creation. Soon, tools such as video cameras, digital cameras, musical instruments, wood-making tools, 3-D printers, and electronic kits will become part of the library collection. And just as libraries have had to make conscious choices regarding which books to circulate, they will soon need to decide whether all of the music studios' keyboards must remain in the library or if a member can check one out.

CHAPTER 8

The New Intelligent Design

You never change things by fighting the existing reality. To change something, build a new model that makes the existing model obsolete.

—R. Buckminster Fuller

With their emphasis on verbal and mathematical skills, rather than designing culture, schools (and even libraries) have actually been shaped by culture. Why? Because these skills have been fundamental to the adaptation and very survival of humans. Libraries and schools usually favor verbal skills by emphasizing literature, narration, storytelling, and poetry, devoting far less attention to math, science, art, music, photography, horticulture, and astronomy. And while, yes, we have books and literature of all sorts devoted to these subjects, it is still unusual to find a library that facilitates learning through art, music, or wellness studios.

In *A Whole New Mind*, author Daniel Pink argues the processing done on the right side of our brains, which results in inventiveness, empathy, and sense of meaning, may become at least as valuable as our verbal and math skills. That's because he believes we are moving from a knowledge and information revolution to a high-touch, high-concept revolution, which he calls the "Conceptual Age." His views follow work done in the seventies and eighties by people such as Bob Samples' "Metaphoric Mind" and Tony Buzan's "Mind Mapping," both of which attempted to better utilize the potential of the right side of the brain.

Pink argues that even though our education systems have favored the left brain, society's current demands require skills better suited for the right brain. With this in mind, Pink's argument for creating balance in our educational system by offering more support for the arts and conceptual thinking appears to have merit. He says the following six senses will become increasingly important in shaping and guiding our lives:

- **Design**: Global competition means that we can now purchase clocks, toasters, or tables for far less. The move now is to create demand for aesthetically pleasing, user-friendly, and fun-to-use designs.

- **Story**: It is our nature as humans to be storytellers. It is simply not enough to bombard people with facts and data, though; we need to communicate through stories. We are drawn to people who can persuade, entertain, and engage our senses with compelling stories.

- **Symphony**: As we move beyond simply focusing on events, we need to put all the pieces together so we can hear the entire symphony. This skill is about seeing the big picture.

- **Empathy**: Logic alone will not suffice in solving our world's complex problems. The high-touch revolution involves gaining a deeper understanding of or empathy for those around us.

Empathy taps the knowledge of friendships and collaborative networks when addressing societal needs.

- **Play**: Seriousness, hard work, and focus will still be needed in the conceptual age, but to think creatively and innovate, we need laughter, humor, and play.

- **Meaning**: As Maslow illustrated in his hierarchy of needs, we need to go beyond material needs to gain fulfillment. We must satisfy our social and self-esteem needs for self-actualization and spiritual connection to take place.

Participatory Learning

When thinking about these emergent shifts, "participatory learning" is one term you'll want to be familiar with. Participatory learning includes the many ways learners (of any age) use new technologies to participate in virtual communities where they can share ideas; comment on one another's projects; and plan, design, implement, advance, or discuss their practices, goals, and ideas together.

The concept of participatory learning is very different from IT (instructional technology), which is usually a predetermined toolkit application that can be institutionalized with little, if any, user discretion, choice, or leverage. IT tends to be top-down, designer-determined, administratively driven, and commercially fashioned. In participatory learning, though, participants can customize the outcomes.

No Right Brain Left Behind

What does all this mean for libraries? Well, it tells us that we need to examine why we exist. If we adopt Lankes' mission statement ("The mission of librarians is to improve society through facilitating knowledge creation in their communities"), then we should do more than simply provide our libraries' patrons with the skills and resources to access information—we should help them create knowledge.

To do this, we'll need to embrace all forms of learning and intelligence, allowing us to move from teachers and librarians to "learning design managers" who facilitate learning. This won't be easy and we won't be able to do it all, but if we focus on improving society by involving our library members, we can create innovative solutions to meet their needs.

ANALOG MEETS DIGITAL

The digital revolution has been enchanting me for the past ten years. I absolutely love useful tools, including the wonderful apps for smartphones and other mobile devices. So when Mike Pelletier, our computer coordinator, proposed we create a research and development (R&D) center for emerging technologies within the library, his ideas resonated with me. Together, we launched the "Connections Project" in 2011 (I'll discuss this more in depth later).

In recent years, two of my colleagues, Doug Tindall and James McMullen, have changed my thinking about the digital revolution and how we can implement and design maker spaces. Neither one set out to convince me; I simply observed them as they helped students with design projects and noticed they both use their experience in applied arts and technology to blend the analog and digital worlds. So much of education today is focused on digital tools and applications that we often lose sight of the fact that the real world comes to us as an analog experience. For example, in the digital world, measurement instruments often provide rapidly switching finite readouts of sound, temperature, light, etc., but in the analog world, you usually see a needle or dial moving across a spectrum. With an analog watch, the website Explain That Stuff (explainthatstuff.com) notes that "...the hand's movements over the dial are a way of representing passing time. It's not the same thing as time itself: it's a representation or an analogy of time." Another entry states, "The same is true of recording sounds with an old-fashioned cassette recorder. The recording you make is a collection of magnetized areas on a long reel of plastic tape. Together, they represent an analogy of the sounds you originally heard."

A Sparkfun.com writer describes exactly this in an article titled "Analog vs. Digital":

> We live in an analog world. There are an infinite amount of colors to paint an object (even if the difference is indiscernible to our eye), there are an infinite number of tones we can hear, and there are an infinite number of smells we can smell. The common theme among all of these analog signals is their infinite possibilities. Digital signals and objects deal in the realm of the discrete or finite, meaning there is a limited set of values they can be.

Digital and analog tools and objects each have advantages and disadvantages. In our quest to go digital, we need to retain and utilize the advantages and useful aspects of analog devices.

DESIGN-BASED THINKING

Project-based learning involves problem solving through design-based thinking. Many excellent books on design and design-based thinking are available, so I won't attempt to provide an in-depth overview; instead, check out this reading list created by the Stanford University Institute of Design: dschool.stanford.edu/resources/dschool-reading-list. (If you're curious, though, my favorite design book about architecture in schools is *The Third Teacher*, which Stanford includes in its list.)

Most design-based thinking models require you to first empathize with your stakeholders to find out their needs; define the problem; ideate viable solutions; create prototypes, starting with low-resolution, cheap, and simple models before moving on to more expensive, elaborate, and full-scale solutions; and then test your final design. This is not a linear process by any means; rather, it's ongoing and can sometimes be visualized as a figure eight.

If you have limited staff, funding, or space, the design-center concept is a good starting point for flipping your library, and quite possibly, your entire school.

WORKING OUTSIDE THE BOX—OR TOOLKIT

Even the wealthiest and best-staffed organization can ill afford to provide full support for every digital device and every software application on the market—the sheer breadth of available tools would be too overwhelming. So most schools' technology departments have a prescribed toolkit listing the hardware and software they can support and are narrowly focused on network issues, with little time allocated for sharing new technologies with the staff and students.

However, if a school were to dedicate a center to emerging technologies that teachers and students could experiment with, including new equipment, tools, and teaching approaches, the R&D team could capture their impressions and feed that information to the IT department and administration. Let's say, for example, a school is considering purchasing tablets for every classroom. The library's R&D center could conduct a test run using one classroom set in several classes before making a final decision, possibly saving the school money before deciding whether or not to make a major school-wide purchase. Most schools have been designed with a fairly small variety of workspaces. Classrooms will vary depending on whether they are built for science classes or English classes. There are usually art rooms, theaters, cafeterias and gymnasiums, but there are rarely large, well-equipped learning spaces for cross-disciplinary collaboration. The library with its size, budget, and staff is a logical place to establish an innovation center with an R&D component.

CREATING AN R&D CENTER FOR EMERGING TECHNOLOGIES

For our libraries to reach their fullest potential, they must become laboratories where we can experiment with new technologies and information sources. To create this kind of learning space, at a minimum, we'll need time, at least one good workspace to conduct in-house research and development, and tools to try. We'll also need a location where teachers and their students can test the most promising approaches to learning or where a community leader can see possible solutions to problems they never knew existed.

The rapid innovation in the world of emerging technologies is exciting, frightening, and confusing. So how can the average person possibly understand which tools are worth the investment of time and money, and which ones are simply bells and whistles promoted through clever marketing? We need an open, honest broker to show us the best new tools for learning, problem solving, innovation, and personal development, and a school library is the perfect setting to serve as testing grounds for emerging technology. Enter the R&D center for emerging technologies.

I find the idea of an R&D center highly appealing, as I think it could potentially transform schools by saving them a considerable amount of money, time, and effort simply by offering a place to test new technologies "in-house" before initiating a school-wide adoption. What's more, ideally, an R&D center would include professional development training for both teachers and students, with collaboration and feedback looping to the curriculum and IT departments.

In my mind, a proper R&D center for emerging technologies would complement the design center but not replace it. The R&D center would focus more on curricular applications of emerging technology and be involved in data collection and the assessment of new tools and skills that teachers and students could use. Universities and corporations are always testing new technologies, but the problem is, they are too far removed from their users. Our libraries' R&D centers, on the other hand, would allow students and teachers to play a role in determining which tools their school acquires to help in the learning process.

In the design center, we problem solve and create new products and projects ranging from musical instruments to origami art. In the R&D center, we purchase new emerging technology such as virtual reality devices and art tablets and then allow teachers and students to use these devices and test their suitability as learning tools.

IT TAKES A VILLAGE

As we begin designing the library of the future, we're faced with this question: "How can we best help others with their personal knowledge creation?" All too frequently, librarians are called upon to be teachers, but our schools already have enough teachers—we need individuals who can support independent learning. "A classroom is not the same thing as a library, and a librarian is not the same thing as a classroom teacher," Lankes writes in *The Atlas of New Librarianship*. "In librarianship, we are often less an instructor than a guide."

Much like a town or a city, a school is a community. Architects and town planners understand the importance of movement, proximity, aesthetics, function, and communication when designing large facilities. With that in mind, school libraries of the future should be centrally located, be easily accessible by all potential members, and incorporate teacher and student input (an essential element). They must be closely integrated with all subject areas, especially the curriculum and IT departments, offering members access to a team of coaches who can facilitate learning.

For the library to have a significant positive impact on learning, all members need to be viewed as stakeholders and must be given a voice in the daily operations. I always cringe a bit when librarians use expressions like, "In my library…" Whose library is it? It is our library, and we all have a stake in how it operates; however, in day-to-day operations, the librarian is tasked with deciding which groups have access and balancing the needs of competing interests in a fair, equitable manner.

The traditional library team isn't adequate for the model I am proposing. To really see fundamental change, the roles of librarians and library assistants will have to change, and other educational professionals will need to be brought on board. I think it's interesting to note that none of my design center colleagues at SAS were ever trained in library and information science. Doug Tindall, who helped create some of our original design studios, gained much of his experience as a general manager for Home Depot. James McMullen, our design center manager, was a shipwright for more than twenty years, designing and creating vessels ranging from kayaks to yachts. Shahrin Aripin, who is now our maker and creation content technician, was trained as an audio engineer. Although all of these individuals are highly skilled, creative, and capable with technology, they are also master craftsmen and designers who love problem solving and hands-on work.

James McMullen, SAS Middle School Library's design center manager, built more than sixty ships and boats while working as a shipwright. He is highly skilled in woodworking, ceramics, art, welding, electronics, and working with students.

In the SAS Middle School Library, we have a good budget, excellent facilities, and good administrative support, all essential elements of success. Libraries involved in maker space activities, project-based learning, and content creation must have skilled staff members, including craftsmen and technicians to effectively facilitate a broad spectrum of learning.

According to the National Center for Education Statistics, there were 98,373 public schools during the 2014-2015 school year. Very few of these schools have innovation centers, learning design studios, R&D centers or cross-disciplinary learning labs, but the vast majority all have libraries. By reimagining, redesigning, and retooling our libraries, we can experiment with new educational approaches and new emerging technologies. Year after year, schools bring in new administrators and new curricular approaches that often take years to implement, and then we start over again. Doesn't it make sense to utilize our school libraries as areas where we can prototype, test, modify, and introduce new ideas before adopting them across an entire school district? The school library can become an agile setting for learning and a catalyst for educational change.

CHAPTER 9

Cool Tools

Evolution of human beings over the past three or four million years can be described in terms of the increasingly sophisticated use of tools.

—*Howard Gardner, PhD,* **Frames of Mind**

O kay, be honest. Did you cheat and just go straight to this chapter? Smart move, because this really is the treasure chest, the tools for the toolkit. Books are meant to be used, and if the only thing you do is try some of the tools in this chapter and never read the remainder of the book, rest assured, my ego will not be bruised. The title for this chapter is a remix taken from *Wired* magazine co-founder Kevin Kelly's excellent *Cool Tools* catalog. (For those of you old enough to remember *The Whole Earth Catalog*, a resource for alternative living in the seventies, Kevin was part of the group that worked with Stewart Brand to create it.)

The design center in the SAS library is a prominent feature and is the largest work area we offer. And although many of our members refer to it as our "maker space," it is more than that. Case in point: We engage students in creative problem solving that can involve the applied arts, which you would, yes, normally find in maker spaces, but we also work with emerging digital technologies. What's more, maker-space models often leave out valuable work in videography and audio recording, so our emphasis on design gives us more latitude.

The key to our design center's success, though, has been its staff members: a creation consultant, James McMullen, and a maker and creation studio technician, Shahrin Aripin. These two individuals are not afraid to try new things and problem solve along with the students. Like James and Shahrin, your design center's team members should serve as educational design consultants, or learning facilitators, and guide and encourage students, while allowing them to try things and make mistakes along the way. The design center's team members and their willingness to learn with the students will always be more important than your equipment or the facility.

Here are some physical features you might want to include in your design center:

- Interactive high-definition projection screens that allow users to manipulate digital data and images

- Technical equipment consoles and operating systems that fold up within the walls when not in use, creating flexible usage of space

- Digital dashboards to track energy use, transportation, book checkouts, etc.

- Ergonomic furniture that can accommodate students using computers and mobile devices

- Unique, easy-to-move shelving that attracts readers to the books

- Noise-resistant flooring with easy-to-clean hygienic surfaces and digital signage and images

- Directed sound to use with multimedia applications, such as TED Talks, which will allow users in one area to hear media without disturbing students involved in quiet reading

- Movable walls, such as glass folding ones, so the space can have multiple uses

- Flexible work and study spaces that include quiet zones for reading and studying as well as more interactive zones for hands-on and collaborative work

- A number of storage spaces for student projects, materials, and equipment

CONSIDERATIONS FOR SELECTING EMERGING TECHNOLOGIES TO INVESTIGATE

Diversity and new connections: How can the introduction of an emerging technology potentially benefit new connections? For example, how would music studios influence other disciplines? Maybe history lessons could incorporate a time period's music.

Development curve: Which technologies are worth investigating in? The NMC Horizon Report and Gartner Inc.'s Hype Cycle for Emerging Technologies are two highly useful sources of information to use when predicting which technologies are likely to take off in the next few years and how education will use them.

Interest factor: What catches your students' and teachers' imaginations? Collect their thoughts on what interests them.

Cost and maintenance factors: How much does the software and hardware cost? How much time and money will it require to maintain? How user-friendly is the technology? How long will it take to learn and implement?

Technology is moving at a faster rate than ever before, and schools cannot afford to re-equip classrooms with the latest and greatest tools without first having proper field testing. This is why an R&D center for emerging technologies is so important. Schools need a place to test new hardware and software before purchasing copies for every classroom, and teachers need time and assistance to see the benefits and liabilities of social networking, cloud computing, geo-tagging, augmented reality, and mobile computing in the classroom.

In the next two "Toolkits," I have grouped potential tools that you can test in the library setting, using two broad categories: physical artifacts (below) and idea starters (page 78).

TOOLKIT OF PHYSICAL ARTIFACTS: REAL AND PHYSICAL FEATURES POSSIBLE WITHIN A LIBRARY

See page 260 for links.

- 360-degree cameras: Allow you to capture setups in learning spaces
- Animated textiles: Will become part of maker spaces
- Augmented reality: Will play a huge role in learning and education
- Digital floors: How to use floors for static or interactive displays
- Directed sound: Allows music and quiet to exist side-by-side
- Egg chairs: Furniture for introverts and those seeking seclusion
- Folding tables with locking wheels: Very handy
- Glass wall dividers: Create new library spaces
- Greenhouse mini: Small plant-growing boxes for horticultural work

TOOLKIT OF PHYSICAL ARTIFACTS (CONT.)

- Hamsters: Hamster homes for a student hamster team to clean
- Keva Planks: Wooden planks for play and designing architecture, art, etc.
- LEGOs: For building, creating, and designing
- Lighting: Ambient, task, accent, etc.
- Life-size cutouts: For authors, fantasy characters, scientists, etc.
- LittleBits: Small electronics kits
- Musical instruments: Possible digital and acoustic instruments
- Nimble: Shows augmented reality with print books
- Phidgets: Electronic components controlled by a personal computer
- Pillows and cushions: Can add comfort and help set a theme
- Plants: Contribute to our naturalistic intelligence
- RFID: Radio frequency systems in libraries
- Robots: Can introduce new elements to a library program
- Solar power: Can charge laptops and mobile devices
- Standing desks: Offer many health benefits
- Ultra-Ever Dry: Ultra-dry, strong, and flexible materials created with nanotech
- Wacom tablet: A sophisticated digital sketching interface
- Walden Zone: Quiet, low-tech spaces to balance interactive spaces
- ZSpace: 3-D images you can enlarge, rotate and take apart

TOOLKIT OF THE IDEATIONAL: CONCEPTS OR IDEAS TO ADAPT AND TRY IN A LIBRARY OR CLASSROOM SETTING

See page 262 for links.

- AI in libraries: Intelligent search engines are just the start
- Appy Hour: Share the best apps with audience participation
- Authors online: Bring authors into your library using Skype
- Balloon Project: Demo physics principles with hot-air balloons
- Big History Project: Access 13.8 billion years of free history
- Blogs: Follow these libraries' and librarians' blogs
- Book trailers: Access countless how-to videos on YouTube
- Brain Rules: John Medina's videos are excellent tools for learning
- Chrome Experiments: Try more than 1,250 highly addictive digital demos and tools
- Content-curation tools: Review this amazing list of resources for curating digital content
- Digital libraries ranking: This ranks the world's best digital libraries
- E-portfolios: These will eventually allow all of us to be librarians
- FutureTimeline.net: A timeline that takes you thousands of years into the future
- Genrification: These are genre images on Pinterest
- Human Library: People are resources, similar to books
- The "Imbecile" and "Moron" Responds: On the Freedoms of Remix Creators
- Infographics: Promote your library using these infographics

TOOLKIT OF IDEA STARTERS (CONT.)

- Learning commons: Read to learn what you should know about the learning commons
- Learning theories map: HoTEL—The Holistic Approach to Technology Enhanced Learning
- Libraries Trending Now: This work by Miguel A. Figueroa is well worth exploring
- Library views: View libraries using Google Street and add yours
- OCLC: This site quantifies the entire library universe
- Padagogy wheel: This shares apps connected to pedagogy
- "Play Is Hard Work": Bud, a teacher, shares his thoughts on play
- "The Power of Play in Learning": Play is essential in libraries
- Visualization methods: Check out flowing data about a variety of topics
- Visualization periodic table: This is an amazing collection of visualization links

CHAPTER 10

Wait, I Never Signed Up for This

You must do the thing you think you cannot do.

—*Eleanor Roosevelt*

What does it mean to be a librarian? We cannot hope to redesign our libraries without first gaining a clear sense of where we are and where we want to go. Once we can do that, we must be able to articulate this mission so that our patrons have a clear understanding of how our roles are evolving to keep pace with the changes in education.

Stereotypes are hard to break, and the image of the shushing librarian giving stern glances to patrons is going to be a tough one to shake. Librarians are often thought of as serious, no-nonsense individuals who focus exclusively on literature and learning. That's in part why, traditionally, literature or history teachers have been drawn to the profession, and as a rule, introverts have been more commonplace than extroverts.

Our libraries' members expect us to be well read and to cherish books and literature in all their varied forms—and rightfully so. But as each day passes, I view my role as more of a learning design specialist in search of the best ways my staff and I can support our school's teachers and students in their learning and teaching. It's not often we librarians are viewed as cutting-edge innovators or radical change agents who experiment with emerging technologies or with problem- or inquiry-based learning, yet that is the direction I suggest our profession moves toward.

OMG! This Could Take a Lifetime to Learn

If you are a librarian, at this point, you may be thinking, "Hold on. I'm doing a good job—I'm a master curator selecting the finest literature. I'm a skilled gardener weeding outdated or irrelevant materials from a superb collection. I'm an information broker providing patrons with easy access, and I'm teaching information literacy skills. How can you expect me to facilitate content creation across all disciplines—music composition, 3-D printing, videography, entrepreneurship, online gaming, and virtual reality as well as thousands of other possibilities—in my little library with my little budget?"

Relax. To start, facilitating knowledge creation is different than teaching. As Lankes explains in *Atlas for New Librarianship,* our role is different than that of teachers: "Librarians don't make learning happen; rather they both create the conditions for learning and fulfill the need for learning on the part of the member." Teachers are being called upon to move from "sage on the stage" to "guide on the side." We need to take teachers' lead and act as learning facilitators who create the proper conditions for learning to take place. We will never have enough money, enough staff, enough time, or enough space to create the ideal conditions, but our job as librarians is to serve as networkers and learning design specialists, and to create the best possible conditions using the resources at our disposal. Our schools have plenty of teachers, and while teaching is one of our duties, it should not be our primary role.

INTEGRATED LEARNING

Education has a long history of hierarchical development and knowledge specialization. It's time for greater integration through cross-disciplinary problem solving. There is no better place than the school library for students to witness the relationship between music and mathematical thinking, the shared subject matter between history and literature, and the common ground between the arts and the sciences.

Ideally, our libraries would effectively facilitate this learning across disciplines and learning styles by establishing a team of learning design coaches. Your team's roster could include coaches for literacy, science and math, art and design, photography and videography, and tech engineering. You may be wondering how in the world schools can afford to hire a team this large and diverse. Chances are pretty high that your school already has teachers who fit these roles. And as schools attempt to institute Google Time and inquiry- or project-based learning, these educators might be able to transition from the classroom to the library's learning settings, community commons, or innovation center. Google Time refers to a type of on-the-job flex-time developed by the 3M Company but made popular through Google. Our school and many others are experimenting with the idea of allowing students time to pursue individual projects that hold a strong personal interest for them. In this manner, students will learn to apply critical thinking and problem solving skills in authentic learning projects that relate to their personal lives and concerns.

To solve the complex global problems of social inequality, climate change, terrorism, air, and water and land pollution, we need people whose expertise spans many different disciplines. Scientists alone cannot solve these problems, nor can politicians, journalists, or filmmakers. Rather, they require systems of collaboration and creative cross-disciplinary thinking. With our help, the school library can become the learning laboratory for this type of life training, where students work on real problems by applying learning concepts in actual hands-on problem solving.

CHAPTER 11

Marketing Is Essential

What a school thinks about its library is a measure of what it feels about education.

–Harold Howe

Given the forces beginning to affect libraries, it is critically important that we quickly communicate the new services our libraries are offering by using marketing and rebranding techniques. Failure to do so could result in our libraries losing even more patrons before they ever hear about our new models of librarianship.

Start by asking your friends—no, don't ask them, ask people you don't know—"When was the last time you went to a library?" The answers may scare you. If it was some time ago, all the great changes our libraries are starting to make may go unnoticed by people who have written us off as passé, out-of-date, or relics.

As you transform your library, publicize the changes you're making to not only entice newcomers but to also bring back people who have abandoned libraries. If you work in a school setting, a beginning-of-the-year library orientation is the perfect time to introduce the changes you've made and help students and teachers understand the new services and support your library offers.

As we delve into this chapter, I'll offer you a few novel activities for creating a new brand, communicating the changes you are making, and delivering new services and offerings to your patrons.

THE MOST POPULAR SOCIAL MEDIA PLATFORMS FOR TEENAGERS IN 2017

1. Snapchat   79%
2. Facebook   76%
3. Instagram 73%
4. Twitter   40%
5. Pinterest 31%

Figure 11.1   *Source: Statistics Portal*

Name Calling

To reflect their change in focus, some libraries are adopting new names such as "community commons," "innovation center," "the hive," or "information hub." I see no harm in this because, as Shakespeare wrote, "A rose by any other name would smell as sweet." On the other hand, Kevin Hennah, a library and retail consultant, feels very strongly that we should retain the name "library," as it is a respected brand.

If you do decide to change your library's name, one word of caution: libraries have established a strong set of core values that we'd be wise to uphold. By remaining members of the ALA and other professional library organizations, we stand a far better chance of retaining the fundamental rights of membership as expressed in the important understandings the organization has developed and negotiated into law.

TOOLKIT OF THE ALA'S CORE VALUES OF LIBRARIANSHIP

- Access: Offer equal and equitable access to information.

- Confidentiality/Privacy: Protect user privacy and confidentiality.

- Democracy: Protect the rights of expression and access to information.

- Diversity: Strive to reflect the diversity of society through a full spectrum of resources.

- Education and Lifelong Learning: Provide lifelong learning services to all.

- Intellectual Freedom: Resist all efforts to censor library resources.

- Preservation: Seek to preserve informational resources.

- Professionalism: Ensure professionally trained personnel are available.

- The Public Good: Libraries are an essential public good.

- Service: Provide the highest levels of service to all library users.

- Social Responsibility: Help in solving the critical problems of society.

Source: American Library Association, bit.ly/2hGgtdg

Weed the Garden of Knowledge

A garden infested with weeds cannot thrive, and, similarly, an old, outdated library collection will not further learning. Books with mold will infect the books next to them. Worn, damaged books will discourage readers by their shabby appearance.

As you retire the books that have served their time and you gain space on your bookshelves, try changing how you display some of the book jackets. We've been told all of our lives not to judge a book by its cover. But we all do it, so stop fighting it and show off the cool new covers that illustrators are designing. You can also gain additional display space by putting up narrow, wall-mounted bookshelves like the ones in the picture below that we purchased from IKEA.

My library highlights staff picks, books that have been read, and new arrivals.

Breakfast Is Served

On the last Friday of each month, the SAS Middle School Library staff hosts breakfast for all ninety-five of the school's teachers. We do this primarily to get teachers into our library so we can highlight our curricular themes, authors, holidays, and special community events. We've been very fortunate to have an administration that pays for these breakfasts, so the money doesn't come out of the library's budget.

These breakfast gatherings are so popular that both the middle school and high school libraries have hosted them for the past twenty years. Here are a few of the many breakfast themes we've highlighted:

- **400th Anniversary of Shakespeare's Life**: We displayed books, quotes, and photos of the Bard and hosted a proper English breakfast.

- **Athletes of the World**: Posters of famous athletes went up alongside smaller picture profiles of faculty members and their athletic achievements.

- **Banned Books**: We displayed the ALA's list of banned books along with explanations about each challenge.

- **East Meets West**: We arranged Western literature and food on one side of the library and Eastern literature and food on the other side.

The ultimate goal of these breakfasts, though, is to create a sense of community and make the library a hub, where events ranging from author visits to drama productions or sporting events are highlighted through books, posters, or even video clips. Our success with this approach has been due not only to the free food, but because it offers our organization's members an opportunity to visit with one another without being in meetings—it's simply a time to socialize and explore the library's displays.

You may be thinking, "Fat chance my school's administration will pay for a breakfast—we are a public library, not a diner." Whoa, you don't have to stage Breakfast at Tiffany's. If you can't get the higher primates to spare any money, simply serve coffee and tea and invite library members to bring in cookies.

BOOK SWAP BOWL

Free books are a good way to attract customers. Take some of the better books you've decided to discard and create a "Book Swap Bowl."

The Book Swap Bowl

Post these instructions for students near the bowl:

Please feel free to swap one or more of your books from home with any of the books in this bowl. For this idea to work, we ask that you only bring in books appropriate for your age group that are in good condition.

We have used this idea for the past ten years with almost zero problems. I must admit, though, that one of the first books we found in the bowl was a beautiful edition of Nietzsche's *Thus Spoke Zarathustra*, a very deep, complex philosophical work that goes way over the heads of middle school students. I now explain to students that we would like them to swap age-appropriate books.

(Side note: You can use whatever container you have on hand for the swap area. My family donated this cool ceramic bowl that was once a water feature in our yard to the library; however, a book box or book basket could certainly achieve the same end.)

GO HOLLYWOOD

Videos are excellent promotional and information tools. According to YouTube company statistics, 4,950,000,000 videos are viewed each day. So challenge students to present their work through project-based learning, and, chances are, they'll choose to make a video with far greater frequency than almost any other medium. Why? Because, well, it seems easy at first—you just point your mobile device at the action and capture something funny, right? However, as students will soon discover, creating interesting videos takes time, patience, and expertise. In fact, it's not uncommon for one minute of quality video to take at least one hour to create. But when done properly, videos can be extremely persuasive, interesting, and compelling. The key is the story; without a storyline, viewers likely will not find the video appealing or persuasive. Videos can also be a highly effective tool when promoting your library's services. Whenever we have a major learning event that we want to share with others, we create a one-minute video to capture the essence. This is far more effective than writing or telling people about it.

AVATARS AT YOUR SERVICE

Using our library video studio, the "Tiger's Eye," we utilized the emerging technology of avatars to facilitate learning by providing our guests with a guided tour. Individuals coming into the library can now go from one numbered station to the next using a smartphone or other mobile device to follow short descriptions of the resources at each station.

Most libraries are understaffed, and the one I work in is no exception. It seems like no matter what my colleagues and I do, there is never enough time in the day and never enough employees to properly help all the students who walk through our doors. That's why we decided to expand our staff by using avatars. By using QR codes with embedded avatar clips, text, photos, and audio tracks, we've set up a complete tour of our library, leading guests from one station to the next.

Our first attempt used our mascot the Koltusky Tiger, aka Mr. T, who was painted by our art teacher, Jeff Koltusky. Mr. T is now our avatar for the Tiger's Eye photo studio. We've made other avatars to serve as entertaining book talks for our members using book jackets and students' voices. You can see a sample of a student-created book talk here: youtu.be/39G0dqCpuq0.

We are now developing avatars who can move about the library and provide members with instructions for using our studios.

CHAPTER 12

The Third Teacher

There are three teachers of children: adults, other children, and their physical environment.

—*Loris Malaguzzi*, The Third Teacher

School communities are much like small towns, complete with politics, competing interests, and competition for real estate. Understandably, teachers from each grade level or academic discipline want to develop the best programs possible for their students, so they compete for money, staff, resources, and physical space.

A school library serves all disciplines and all grade levels, so it must be highly flexible, agile, and collaborative so it can meet everyone's needs. Therefore, it usually has a large footprint and a large budget. However, once a school's staff and faculty begin viewing the library as underutilized, it's not long before someone suggests taking over a small slice of the cake (or, in this case, library space) to accommodate an important new position or program or even just to store their stuff. Many schools are choosing to build maker spaces separate from libraries, but I think this is a lost opportunity; not only can the library space be used for maker activities, but library staff members can also serve as mentors and coaches working side by side with technicians, designers, and engineers.

I've visited several innovative schools on the American West Coast, and I've been struck by how many have decided to close their libraries in favor of creating maker spaces. From my vantage point, the two are not mutually exclusive, but instead mutually inclusive, in that every library should be a place of innovation.

SHELTER FROM THE STORM

If you want to transform your library, the first thing you must do is look at the basics. Abraham Maslow theorized that, before we can reach up to our higher needs of wisdom and self-actualization, we must first take care of our most basic needs, including safety, food, and shelter.

As students, teachers, and human beings, we are shaped and influenced by each other and the environments in which we work, study, and live. Part of our responsibility as librarians is to provide a learning space where members will feel accepted, comfortable, supported, and safe.

Chris Bourg, MIT's director of libraries, is quoted in an article titled "Is the Library the New Public Square?" as saying, "I want the libraries to be that space where the students and the community can feel that those riches—the science that happens here, the learning that happens here—that they are a part of that...." I want that too, for so many reasons, not the least of which is that students who may not fit in with social circles often find libraries as a refuge and an emotionally safe zone.

LEARNING TO TAKE A FRESH LOOK

The more time we spend in one setting, the more we can become so accustomed to our surroundings that our observations can become a bit static. In *On Looking*, dog cognition expert Alexandra Horowitz, PhD, gains a fresh look at her familiar surroundings by taking eleven walks, each with an individual from a different profession who can offer a unique perspective on observation. Perhaps we can do something similar and enlist the help of our library's students, parents, faculty, and staff, allowing each one to offer us a new perspective on our space. After all, as stakeholders, they should be involved in helping us enhance our library's comfort and learning potential. It's important to take frequent walks with others in libraries to observe and take note of what captures people's interest and attention.

When you walk into a library, what physical evidence do you look for to determine the type of learning that is taking place? How are people using the spaces? Talk to your stakeholders. Ask why certain locations are popular and other areas are underused or in need of a makeover. What suggestions can patrons offer? How would you describe the room's style? Is it formal or informal? Is it institutional or homey? What is the comfort level? How does the air smell? How are the sound and lighting? These are all small things that play big roles in the learning environment.

You might be thinking, "I'm not an architect or an interior designer, so how can I determine or even have an influence on a space that was designed as part of the overall school environment?" True, you will more than likely face institutional restrictions, but, hopefully, your school's administration will listen if you propose ways to enhance students' learning, health, and safety through better interior design. And while there is no one-size-fits-all template for the library (or even the classroom) of the future, librarians can sample their patrons' opinions and experiment with environments to find the ones most conducive to learning.

TIME, SPACE, MONEY, AND PERMISSION

Now, let's suppose you identify some tangible changes you think could improve your library's learning environment. You might be asking yourself, "How much time and money can I afford to spend on this issue?" And if you finally manage to solve the time and money problems, "How can I convince my administrator to go along with the changes?" These are all valid concerns that require unique solutions dependent upon your school and your educational community, but remember this: you are in a partnership with your library members. Your chances of gaining support will be much better if you can provide evidence for improved learning.

Consider the following before you start:

- What is your budget?

- What kinds of learning are you trying to support?

- How much space do you have?

- How many students occupy that space?

- How can you enlist the support of your teachers, students, and administrators?

- How much time can you spend on this? (Tip: even a small amount helps.)

MI CASA ES SU CASA

Depending upon your community's needs and interests, you could create a wide variety of zones, studios, and learning spaces within your library. While schools tend to be improving their overall look, most still have an institutional feel, with fluorescent lighting, conservative structural designs, and standardized furnishings. But considerable brain-based research is being done, and much of it is pointing toward the idea that homelike environments tend to promote learning. Concordia University in Portland, Oregon, posted an article titled "5

Ways to Design a School for Brain-Based Learning," discussing why and how homey layouts promote interaction, comfortable furniture reduces stress, bright colors stimulate the brain, seating arrangements foster face-to-face interaction, and immersive settings allow hands-on experiences.

My personal mission is to transform institutional settings into areas that look and feel more like home, a nice hotel, or a resort. I don't believe we need to suffer in bad environments to learn; rather, we learn best when we feel safe, comfortable, and at home.

Okay, take a break, go to Spotify, and play "My House" by Flo Rida.

The Living Room

AGILE OR PURPOSE-BUILT?

When we look at improving a library, we always have to consider the stakeholders' unique needs. For example, libraries for young children will need to be more concerned with safety, whereas those serving older students should provide adequate access to technology. One of the ways we can identify our learners' needs is to simply ask them how they learn best—"Do you work best in small groups or on your own?" "Do you fall asleep when you read on a pillow or do you really get into the story better when you are more comfortable?"—and then observe.

As we go up the educational ladder, library studios for subjects such as videography and photography or music will need to be more purpose-built, while you'll find other areas can be more flexible and agile, allowing for a wider spectrum of activities and to support several types of learning.

Case in point: musicians perform best in purpose-built concert halls that take acoustics, seating, and experience-enhancing aesthetics into account. Artists work best in art studios that have proper lighting, allow for adventurous experimentation, and are equipped with the proper brushes, canvases, and paints. And in the same vein, students tend to learn best in areas allowing for innovation and creativity, as well as collaboration, communication, and critical thinking.

In their book *The Language of School Design*, architects Prakash Nair and Randall Fielding outline eighteen "learning modalities" (see the "Toolkit" on the opposite page) that, they believe, the physical school can support. As schools adopt teaching methods that involve more independent study, more peer-to-peer interaction, and more work with emerging technologies, our learning settings will need to accommodate these changes.

Nair and his colleagues recently assessed our school's overall facilities and highlighted our library as one of the best-designed spaces. Of course, my colleagues and I were happy to receive the compliment, but we were even more eager to learn how we could make our library better. So when someone asked me, "When do you plan to be finished with the changes in the library?" I replied, "Never. We want to keep changing and adapting to needs, ensuring we have a dynamic environment, not a static one." I didn't mention it then, but we also want to minimize too much disruption for our students so they know where to find things and

TOOLKIT FOR LEARNING MODALITIES

- Independent study
- Peer tutoring
- Team collaborative work in small- and mid-size groups (two to six students)
- One-on-one learning with the teacher
- Lecture format with the teacher or outside expert at center stage
- Project-based learning
- Technology-based learning with mobile computers
- Distance learning
- Research via the Internet with wireless networking
- Student presentations
- Performance- and music-based learning
- Seminar-style instruction
- Community service learning
- Naturalist learning
- Social and emotional learning
- Art-based learning
- Storytelling (floor seating)
- Learning by building—hands-on learning

Source: The Language of School Design

can feel comfortable in the spaces they have grown used to. With this in mind, as ours have, your visitors may find it helpful if you have a map of your zones at your library's entrance, like the one below developed by Doug Tindall.

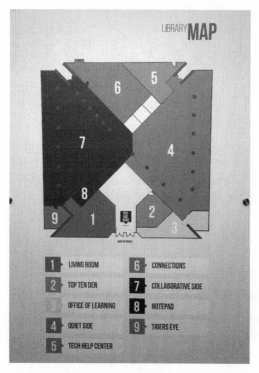

CAMPFIRES IN CYBERSPACE

Almost any library architect or design consultant will tell you that modern libraries must be both agile and flexible. I couldn't agree more, but part of that agility is including purpose-built areas capable of handling specific needs, such as a recording studio or photo lab.

In his article "Campfires in Cyberspace" (which is essentially a remix of anthropologist Gregory Bateson's tale of archetypal learning environments), educational consultant David Thornburg, PhD, proposes four types of physical settings that, he says, are conducive to learning:

Campfire: This first setting is where individuals can sit in a circle designed for group discussion. The key is for members to feel included and involved in the group process.

A campfire setting

The Watering Hole: The second setting is the watering hole, where people can informally gather to have a beverage or a snack and share ideas in a spontaneous, unstructured way. Great ideas often emerge from watering holes, such as pubs or coffee shops, and many libraries have seen success with established zones for cafés or coffee shops.

A watering hole setting

Caves: The third setting is a "cave," since it provides a space where students can work in solitude and focus on private study. Caves serve as places where individuals can collect their thoughts, focus on difficult subjects, enjoy entertainment via books or music on headphones, or even sleep, if needed.

A cave setting

Mountaintop: Finally, the mountaintop area is where a large audience can gather for a performance, speech, or presentation. In a library setting, this space often requires a projection system and appropriate sound and lighting, but it may also be an enclosed theater, or simply a large space equipped with the ability to darken the room and highlight major events.

Having areas that can be closed off or opened using glass walls or movable partitions help improve a space's agility and flexibility immensely. I've found chairs and folding tables on wheels are highly functional, and if chosen with care, can add to a library's modern and attractive look.

A mountaintop setting

CIVIC SPACES AND SHARED OWNERSHIP

As members of the school community, teachers are expected to reserve times for special events or for classes to visit the library, and they make arrangements with our staff through Google booking forms. Our booking procedures allow us to prepare seating arrangements, materials, and equipment that might be needed. Individual students or small groups may also make bookings to reserve our specialized studios. With over 1,000 guests per day, setups, take-downs, and bookings are essential to avoid conflicts over the use of space, materials, and equipment.

In *The Atlas of New Librarianship*, David Lankes makes a useful distinction between public and civic spaces:

> *True facilitation means shared ownership...A researcher called the public library a public space. I corrected her. The public library is a civic space. What is the distinction? A public space is not truly owned. It is an open space. Things in the public domain, for example, are free to use and reproduce. A civic space, on the other hand, is a regulated space on behalf of the*

public. That means it is beholden to a whole raft of policy and law. A group can gather in a public space. They have to have permission to do so in a civic space, and that permission must be given in an equitable and nondiscriminatory way...It represents a partnership between a member and the librarian. It is a jointly owned enterprise.

Y'All Come Back, Ya Hear?

Librarians sometimes fail to appreciate the fact that we have the unique ability to make things happen through "convening power." "We can pull together groups for all sorts of purposes and conversations," Lankes says. "We can be the ones to get the ball rolling on important issues."

Libraries can host more than just author visits—they can become the hub of a learning institution or a neighborhood community by hosting events across the curriculum. And by making our libraries inviting, welcoming spaces, groups will be more likely to want to book their events there. Figure 12.1 features just a sampling of the events my library has facilitated and that your library may be able to host as well. Just as my staff and I continually do, I encourage you to strive to make the library you work in the heart of your school or community and the hub of innovation.

The Classroom of the Future

In 2014, through a partnership with InfoComm, Singapore's National Institute of Education (NIE) created a model for what it considered the "classroom of the future." The prototype incorporated possible design features using the best, most current technology, resulting in a dynamic, modern space. NIE continues to publish research on classroom design and its impact on learning. Their idea of creating an experimental classroom is worth pursuing.

CONFERENCES	SPECIAL EVENTS	WORKSHOPS & MEETINGS
Wellness conference	Strings ensemble	New student orientations
Google summit	Visiting authors	An Hour of Code
Facilities safety conference	Egyptian museum	Faculty meetings
Special Ed Network	CSI crime scenes	Poetry café
Math Olympiad	Yearbook photos	MAP testing
Strengths Finder	Science hot-air balloons	"Appy Hour"
Telluride Film Festival	Spanish weather reports	Info lit library resources
Chinese language conference	Tuesdays with TED	Money talk/personal finance
Summer school	National History Day	Internet safety workshop
Apple leadership	Science water projects	Peer counsel meetings
Talent show auditions	Caring for Cambodia	Social studies ME peace
Digital citizenship	Figurine painting	Singapore library network

Figure 12.1

Schools can very easily build their own "classroom of the future" inside their libraries, offering community members an area conducive to creating and testing innovative learning spaces. And as they experiment, students and teachers could offer ideas and suggestions for ways to improve the setting, resulting in new iterations that serve as catalysts for change throughout the school.

Think about this: to what extent or in what ways does the library you work in support, enable, or constrain possibilities for these forms of learning? How could classrooms or libraries be more flexibly designed so as to support different learning modalities? And if we want to promote the kind of skill development and agility the twenty-first century will require, how can we design more flexible spaces to support such teaching and learning?

DESIGN-BASED THINKING

In his 2007 article "33 Educational Design Principles for Schools and Community Learning Centers," educational planner and architect Jeffery Lackney, PhD, says that by applying as many of his thirty-three principles to school design as appropriate, "We can optimize the school and its surrounding community as an effective setting for learning." Schools focus considerable time and energy on curriculum and teaching methods, but we devote very little to designing the environment in which we interact with our students.

In the "Toolkit for Design," I've listed a number of features to pay special attention to as you examine the physical settings in which you facilitate, learn, and work.

TOOLKIT FOR DESIGN

- Maximize collaboration in school planning and design.
- Consider your home a template for your library.
- Design libraries that feel comfortable and safe.
- Cluster learning areas.
- Provide space for sharing learning resources.
- Provide resource-rich, well-defined activity pockets.
- Provide studios to support project-based learning.
- Encourage educational leadership by decentralizing administrative spaces.
- Establish a community forum.
- Offer a community conferencing space.
- Create privacy niches.
- Weave together virtual and physical learning spaces.
- Maximize natural and full-spectrum lighting.
- Design healthy buildings.
- Design for appropriate acoustics.
- Allow for transitional spaces between indoor and outdoor spaces.

Walk and Talk Like an Architect

Librarians can sometimes be dismissed as fussy bookish types who don't understand the work of architects and designers, so having some understanding of the basic guidelines for good environmental design can prove helpful when outlining your plans.

Here are some of the terms I've found most useful when designing our school's library:

Indoor Air Quality (IAQ): Sets down procedures and guidelines for determining air quality standards inside buildings

Indoor Environmental Quality (IEQ): Affects people's performance, whether they are in work, home, or learning environments

Leadership in Energy and Environmental Design (LEED) Guidelines: Provides architects with guidelines for creating more energy-efficient buildings

POE Post-Occupancy Survey: Helps determine if IEQ standards have been met

Sick Building Syndrome (SBS): Deals with the causes and prevention of toxic conditions that can develop in buildings due to improper construction materials or methods

Temperature: Studies are finding that air's temperature and quality can affect students' learning performance

Source: "Indoor Environmental Quality of Classrooms and Student Outcomes: A Path Analysis Approach"

Future Libraries: Workshops Summary and Emerging Insights by Arup University offers an excellent analysis of the impact of the digital revolution on future library design. In the words of the authors:

> *Robotics and big data, when applied both to spatial design and to information management, have the potential to disrupt the traditional balance between storage and collaborative spaces. This can provide opportunities to create more livable and*

diverse solutions. Such diversity will be key to achieve a good level of flexibility, which will accommodate the demands and aspirations of hyper-diverse users. The challenge for librarians will lie in a deeper understanding of users' needs, in order to provide them with relevant information. Librarians will need to consider new skills, greater collaboration and a multi-disciplinary approach to their profession.

TOOLKIT FOR LEARNING SPACES
See page 265 for links.

- **BREEAM**: Energy, health, innovation, and sustainability in building design
- **Green Star**: Australian best practice benchmarks for sustainability
- **Learning Space Toolkit**: Includes a road map, needs assessment, and spaces types
- **Learning Space Rating System**: The nuts and bolts of architectural planning

CHAPTER 13

Building a Smart *and* Intelligent Library

I believe life is an intelligent thing: that things aren't random.

—Steve Jobs

Cities around the world are beginning to employ video cameras, electronic counters, automated LED lights, and sensors, creating an intelligent environment that responds to human needs. Today, we have smart homes and smart cities, and soon, we may even have smart countries. In fact, in 2015, Singapore launched its Smart Nation initiative, providing residents in selected neighborhoods with data on transportation, energy usage, and resource management. This data in turn allows city designers to best meet community needs through improved infrastructure such as new roads, better signage, better lighting, etc.

Smart cities integrate a variety of information and communication solutions to manage a community's assets in an attempt to improve citizens' quality of life through technology. Cities around the world are already taking advantage of smart technology to better manage their power grids, water resources, transportation, and hospitals, and many have instituted smart parking, smart roads, smart lighting, air pollution detection, and smart energy grids. We'll increasingly see this Internet of things in our daily lives, and, hopefully, it will provide us with a better world. (Libelium offers a good sampling of smart technology in its article "50 Sensor Applications for a Smarter World.")

But what if we were to take smart technology and incorporate it into a library setting? What might a "smart library" look like? Here is one scenario to consider...

Envision this: before you enter the library, you see a touchscreen catalog for quick searches and a large LED screen showing covers of books just added to the collection. Once you pass through the front entrance, a video camera takes your photo and adds it to a collage of the library's current visitors on a nearby screen. If you'd prefer, you can delete the photo at a nearby computer terminal.

Near the entrance you see a circulation desk with an automated checkout system and a staff member to answer questions; however, you may prefer to ask for assistance from Jibo, the personal robot sitting alongside the library assistant. The library's air conditioning, lighting, and air quality are all monitored and automatically adjusted to create an optimal learning environment. And in certain sections of the library are speakers in the ceiling providing directed music that only you can hear if you are directly underneath one. You may also see a wide variety of projections screens like those depicted in Cornings video "A Day Made in Glass". You get the feeling that the library is a learning hub for the school, bringing in new ideas to share.

The library's books and equipment all have electronic tags equipped with radio-frequency identification (RFID), allowing the librarians to easily locate materials and return them to their proper place. Using the library catalog, you create and access your personal account and library statistics providing you with helpful information about your own personal usage and advice on future books you might want to read.

With sensors, cameras, usage information on data use, robotics, and other features possibly becoming part of the library environment, librarians and patrons will be faced with issues of privacy versus sharing of public and personal information. These issues are becoming readily apparent in our daily lives. The library is a safe environment to test out the boundaries of privacy and sharing, and with careful thought and planning, we can allow for a dialog about the direction we want our social norms to take.

Big Brother?

As you were reading the last section, did you feel the lurking presence of Big Brother looking over your shoulder? Yes, having technology that tracks your whereabouts and anticipates your every need can also be used to control your actions and even manipulate you. And as smart technology evolves, so will the tension between its benefits and its invasion of our personal privacy.

I have to admit, I do like the genius programs Amazon and Spotify have set up to help me find recommendations, but I also worry I am losing some control and becoming more boxed-in by systems that try to anticipate my needs and desires. Perhaps we need to confront these issues head-on by carefully looking at the smart devices and the Internet of things that we bring into our lives, while staying vigilant not to become Luddites, who miss out on the advantages and pleasures such systems can offer. We need to ensure our libraries have tech-free areas or "Walden Zones," where members can unplug and escape the world of push-and-pull technology.

To support our students' understanding of this conflict between personal privacy and technology, we must involve them in discussions, as it will continue playing a larger and larger role in everyone's lives. We cannot shield and protect them at the same time. And in the same way that libraries have guarded against the censorship of literature, we must also guard against the censorship of new technology. As librarians, we should look at what is being pushed onto us and evaluate what is socially useful and what is a waste of time and possibly even harmful. Students will inevitably be exposed to technology and social engineering through capitalism outside of school, so we must bring the issues into the school so they have time for reflection and evaluation.

PROJECT ZERO

In a previous life, I worked as a school counselor and trained as a school psychologist. In 1996, my employer gave me the opportunity to take a one-year sabbatical at Harvard University. My wife Kate joined me and completed her master's degree in educational administration. Over the course of the year, I designed three internships, which allowed me to work as an interviewer for undergraduate admissions, a career counselor in the School of Education, and a librarian at Widener Library. One of my projects at Widener was to rewrite a training manual for library employees at the circulation desk. The original version written by my predecessor had a title that I liked, "Alice in Widenerland," so I kept it for the new manual.

Each day, when Kate and I walked from our apartment to her classes and to my work, we passed the Harvard's Project Zero building. I knew of Howard Gardner's work in multiple intelligences and found it to be a far better model for explaining learning than the established g factor IQ tests, which I was tasked with administering years earlier as a school psychologist intern at the University of Oregon. Gardner and his colleagues at Project Zero conducted numerous studies and identified eight forms of intelligence or learning styles.

As any teacher will confirm, students have many different learning modalities. As humans, we don't all think, act, or learn in the same way, yet schools are moving oh-so-slowly in finding ways to individualize and personalize the learning experience. We need to find ways to differentiate learning to better support and nourish all forms of human intelligence.

For a quick look at your own modalities of thought, take this quick multiple intelligences quiz: bit.ly/2imTtgf.

LEARNING DESIGN STUDIOS

My library staff and I are always looking for ways in which we can better support all these forms of learning by creating purpose-built "learning design studios."

Mark Baildon, PhD, of Singapore's National Institute of Education, and I wrote an article titled "Designing Classrooms of the Future," in which we documented the effects of classroom design on student learning. In our observations, we found that almost everything in a student's physical surroundings, including the lighting, temperature, air quality, furniture, ceilings, walls, and floors, can have a remarkable influence on human behavior and learning. While educational studies focus heavily on curriculum and teaching methods, little attention is paid to the physical environment and its effect on learning outcomes.

GOING FROM SMART TO INTELLIGENT

Most educators are uncomfortable discussing the issue of intelligence—we've been taught to take an egalitarian approach to education and rightfully so. When we engage in conversations about our students' or colleagues' intelligence, we are walking on thin ice. Nevertheless, educational and cognitive psychologists have relied on IQ testing as important tools for measuring learning.

It may or may not come as a surprise, then, to learn that of all the psychological assessment tools available, intelligence tests have the highest levels of statistical validity and reliability, far higher than personality and even achievement tests. The problem with these tests, though, lies in the fact that the two main tools used to assess intelligence, the Stanford-Binet and the Wechsler intelligence scales, measure a far narrower construct than we normally think of when discussing intelligence. In recent years, the Wechsler tests, the current standard, have arranged their subtests into clusters describing different types of intelligence.

If we, as librarians, create smart libraries, we could potentially collect useful statistics about students' studio and equipment usage and determine where intelligent systems are needed to help users to find information or assistance. Books and equipment can now be tagged with RFIDs to find things more easily, and LED screens can display messages about community events and notices. And when we spot trends, we can create and share videos to communicate those trends with our users.

Libraries allow us an opportunity to break out and try new designs within our communities. Since so many different types of people enter our libraries for so many different purposes, we need to provide flexible, agile spaces to accommodate all types of learning. Using Gardner's multiple intelligences model, my colleagues and I have created learning design studios, or zones, designed to highlight and facilitate learning in multiple areas.

It's important to note that one learning activity often involves two or more intelligences simultaneously. And while we've grouped our learning support based on the forms of intelligence applied, you could very easily use a number of other possible models instead of this paradigm. For our purposes, though, determining if a particular tool or learning activity belongs in one studio instead of another is not as crucial as providing patrons convenient access to these tools.

LEARNING DESIGN STUDIOS TO SUPPORT MULTIPLE INTELLIGENCES

Name	Function	Intelligence Supported
Top Ten Den	Reading room	Linguistic
Design Center	Project design	Logical/mathematical
Note Pad	Recording studio	Musical
Tiger's Eye	Photography studio	Spatial
Wellness Zone	Movement and exercise	Bodily-kinesthetic
Living Room	Highlights nature	Naturalistic
Pier Point	Self-understanding	Interpersonal and intrapersonal

Figure 13.1

If you have limited space or resources—and we all have such limits—you'll need to choose which types of zones will work best in your setting. It's not important whether or not you adopt the multiple intelligences model; the important thing is that you are willing to support and facilitate all types of learning.

When my colleagues and I created a music studio in the library, I was a bit worried about parent, teacher, or administrator pushback. I didn't worry about the students—I knew they would be flexible thinkers willing to try something new. However, I did envision being cornered by a stern English teacher, questioning what I was doing placing a music studio in this shrine to literature. I also imagined a parent ranting about my wasting precious library funds on wild ideas that had nothing to do with libraries. I needed to provide the "why" for this endeavor—why would we think a music studio was okay in a library setting? I had many thoughts, but I seized on Gardner's theory of multiple intelligences, and I realized that by including a music studio in our library, my colleagues and I were helping to facilitate musical intelligence. The criticisms I expected never happened; instead, we had critical conversations about learning. Students', staff members', and parents' acceptance of the music studio gave our library team the confidence we needed to push forward and find even more ways to support the other forms of intelligence.

Gardner's multiple intelligences model has allowed us to rethink our whole approach to library services and learning options. I want to stress that this option comes to me naturally based on my experience and training as a school counselor and school psychologist. The multiple intelligences model may not work for you or your community (I will address this further in "Chapter 25: Paradigm Shift"), and that's okay. I believe you can successfully use the ideas I present in this book without ever touching the multiple intelligences theory, as long as you have a logical rationale for why you are introducing these changes.

CHAPTER 14

We Are Storytellers

We tell ourselves stories in order to live.
—*Joan Didion*, The White Album

I believe the most important form of intelligence for adaptation and survival in our world today is linguistic intelligence, which includes reading, writing, comprehending complex abstract ideas, problem solving with language, and seeking understanding through language. So if you want to boost your IQ, read as much as possible.

Not only does reading boost your vocabulary, it also improves your critical thinking, spurs your creativity, broadens your horizons, increases your general knowledge, and takes you to places you've never imagined. What's more, vocabulary is the most stable of all subtests on the Wechsler and Stanford-Binet intelligence scales, and this form of intelligence plays a pivotal role in how we make sense of the world.

As society evolves and artificial intelligence plays a greater role in our lives, it is possible one of the other forms of intelligence will become the kingpin. Whatever happens in the future, though, tomorrow's libraries will continue to be rich reservoirs of verbal knowledge, though they will not rely solely upon books and other written documents.

IREAD, ISPEAK, IWRITE

In *Frames of Mind*, Gardner describes linguistic intelligence as the "ability to analyze information and create products involving oral and written language such as speeches, books, and memos." He goes on to say that linguistic intelligence involves "a sensitivity to the meaning of words, the order among words and the sound, rhythms, inflections, and meter of words (e.g., poetry)."

He says a person's ability to read, write, tell stories, and memorize words all contributes to linguistic intelligence. Gardner identifies four important aspects of linguistic knowledge:

- Rhetoric helps us convince others of a course of action.

- Language serves as a tool to remember information.

- Language is useful as a teaching tool for providing explanations.

- Language can reflect upon itself to explain its own activities (meta-linguistics).

This area receives significant support from the traditional library model and the general curriculum, so it is tied most closely to the general intelligence that's crucial for all forms of thinking and problem solving. In their traditional form, our libraries do a pretty decent job of supporting linguistic intelligence, but we're not as successful in our support of Gardner's other forms of intelligence.

THE TOP TEN DEN

Since libraries already focus a great deal of their attention on linguistic intelligence, you might wonder why I felt the need to create a special studio to support this learning mode in SAS Middle School's library. One reason is because I want to highlight it as one of the eight forms of intelligence but not as the only form libraries can support. Libraries can be large and intimidating, so having a dedicated space showcasing the "best books" makes it easy for patrons to locate good reads with little effort. Plus, I believe marketing books is essential in promoting reading.

Premala Sekaran, pictured here in the Top Ten Den, has worked in university, high school, and middle school libraries. She is our cataloger, purchasing agent, volunteer coordinator, and reference librarian.

GETTING STARTED

On a basic level, you could start with:

- A dedicated space with comfortable seating

- A nice selection of "best books" categorized by genre or subject area, such as history, science, etc.

- A modest amount of shelving that can hold ten books for each category

- Signage for instructions and categories

Start by simply highlighting some of each genre's best books, listing about a hundred for each. When creating these lists, my staff and I rely on a number of different sources, including the ALA's and Young Adult Library Services Association's (YALSA) lists, award winners, Amazon, Goodreads, LibraryThing, Shelfari, and of course teacher and student recommendations. We knew students would notice changes in this collection, so we keep it dynamic by replacing the top ten selections for each genre the first week of each month. We also added signage to encourage users to take these books off the shelves and check them out.

Due to our large number of visitors each day and relatively small staff, we hope to create an avatar for each specialty to help guide and instruct patrons. We are considering adding a Shakespeare avatar to our Top Ten Den to talk to students about the value of good literature and explain how we select and display our best books. In his own words, he would express some concern that none of his books are in this month's display and encourage visitors to check out the books.

GOING A FEW STEPS FURTHER

You don't need a separate room for your best books selections, but a quiet area designed for readers certainly helps. We designed our Top Ten Den to feature the best books from our collection's major genres. Identifying and labeling books by genre has been a great way to encourage reading, but it does have its advantages and disadvantages. Genres can help readers locate literature that appeals to their interests; however, certain books can occupy a place in more than one genre, making the classification difficult. For this reason, we still arrange our books according to the Dewey Decimal System, but we've also created online genre categories and placed genre labels on the spine of each book.

There are no set rules for *genrefication* or one thesaurus to turn to for genre terms, but you will find many sources on the Internet and in books to help you with the process. Several years ago, when deciding upon our genres, we did some research and then collaborated with our school's English teachers. We decided to use the categories of adventure, classics, family, fantasy, graphic novels, historical fiction, horror, humor, mystery, realistic fiction, romance, science fiction, and sports.

Once you've tagged and labeled your entire fiction collection, changing your categories is a daunting task. That said, if I were to make changes now, I would probably eliminate "westerns" and combine "family/romance" and "horror/mystery."

We encourage students to take books off the display shelves, to check them out, and then, as books are borrowed, we replace them with new ones from the genres' lists. On the first Monday of each month, we put up a whole new set of books in every category to keep interest high and the display dynamic.

BIBLIOTHERAPIST

As a former school counselor, I would relish the opportunity to become a bibliotherapist: someone who can size up a person, listen to their concerns, and then recommend the perfect book. Some well-read librarians have a knack for this, but, unfortunately, I'm not one of them—I read rather slowly, preventing me from having a vast reserve of books in my memory to draw upon. Even the most prolific reader cannot hope to read the 30,000 books in the modest library where I work, so sometimes shortcuts can come in handy. If you're like me, the "Toolkit of Book Recaps" (below), featuring sites that offer quick overviews of classics and other works will come in handy. You can share all of the sites I've listed with middle school students and older, with the exception of Wisecrack's Thug Notes, which is very well done but uses pretty crude language.

TOOLKIT
OF BOOK RECAPS
See page 269 for links.

- 60second Recap: Text and videos on contemporary and ancient classics

- Booknotes: Serious sixty-minute video discussions by authors, focusing on one book

- CliffsNotes: The granddaddy of them all offers no-nonsense analyses of literature

- CrashCourse: Highly innovative educational content

- Horrible Histories: Patterned after the book series in video cartoon form

- SparkNotes: Translations, explanations, and reviews of fiction and nonfiction

- Wisecrack's Thug Notes: Funny (usually sexual) and rude video reviews of classics

TOOLKIT FOR
FINDING THE BEST BOOKS

See page 266 for links.

- Amazon: Look up a book you like and read their suggestions.

- Booklists by Age: Multnomah County Public Library has put together great lists.

- Booksource: Search using Lexile levels.

- Common Sense Media: Find best book lists for kids and families.

- Cool Tools: Access dictionaries, word walls, tagging galaxies, and more.

- Goodreads: This is one of the top book platforms.

- Lexile: Find the Right Book for You!: Students can find "just right" books.

- Literature Map: Search this very fun, interactive map of authors.

- Mrs. ReaderPants: Explore themes ranging from bullying to resistant readers.

- OCLC WorldCat Genres: OCLC's world catalog is a wonderful source.

- What Should I Read Next?: This links to Goodreads and helps readers to find books similar to their favorites.

- Wikipedia – Great Books: Research the classics.

- YA (and Kids!) Books Central: See the most-reviewed, highest-rated, and most popular books.

- YourNextRead: Type in a title and get some good suggestions.

TOOLKIT FOR BOOK AWARDS
See page 267 for links.

- Agatha Awards (mystery)
- Bailey's Women's Prize for Fiction
- Bram Stoker Awards (horror)
- Caldecott Medal
- Christy Awards (Christian)
- Culinary Classics Awards
- Edgar Awards (mystery)
- Hugo Awards (science fiction/fantasy)
- Indie Bestseller Award List
- International Horror Guild
- James Tiptree, Jr., Literary Award (science fiction/fantasy)
- James Beard Foundation Awards (culinary)
- John W. Campbell Memorial Award (science fiction)
- Lambda Literary Awards (LGBT)
- Macavity Awards (mystery)
- Man Booker Prize
- Mystery Writers of America
- National Book Awards
- National Book Critics Circle Awards
- Nebula Awards (science fiction/fantasy)
- Nero Award (mystery)
- Newbery Medal

TOOLKIT FOR BOOK AWARDS (CONT.)

- Nobel Prize in Literature
- PEN/Malamud Award for Short Fiction
- Pulitzer Prize
- Quill Awards
- RITA Awards (romance)
- Shamus Awards
- Spur Award (history and western)

JOIN THE WALL OF FAME

Each year, we photograph our school's new teachers and add them to the library's Wall of Fame. Though this idea has been around for ages, it is still very popular. We use software from the ALA to create cool backgrounds and encourage teachers to dress the part and highlight their personal reading interests.

Here is a sample note we send out to teachers:

Dear Teachers,

We invite you to join the Wall of Fame. Our library staff will create a beautiful "READ" poster, which we'll then print and frame. The students love seeing their teachers like movie stars, and it helps us to promote books and reading. Our photo studio will be open all day this Thursday and Friday, so feel free to stop by anytime between 8 a.m. and 3 p.m.

Bring: A book you like and any props or costumes you'd like to wear.

Help: See a library staff member; we will help you find a good book and maybe even a good prop.

Hollywood has its stars....　　　　　　And we have ours...

Support reading, model literacy, be cool. Join the Wall of Fame.

READING NINJAS

My staff and I know avid readers love talking about books they've read with their friends, so we founded the "Reading Ninjas," a club specifically for students who want to learn about great books and then share that information with their friends and other students seeking help. We tested the idea to see if this group of enthusiastic readers could successfully attract other readers their age and convey the idea that reading is not only enjoyable but also cool and popular. We found that we needed confident readers who were popular with their peers for this approach to work.

Our plan was to use the Ninjas to connect with all kinds of readers, including reluctant readers and those who need their peers' support and encouragement to become more active readers. We asked experienced language arts teachers to serve as the Reading Ninjas' sponsors to help the Ninjas select "just right" books to fit each reader's reading level and reading style. And since no one wants to be told what to read, we taught the Reading Ninjas how to engage in conversations with their "patrons" or "customers" and then find books to fit their needs and interests.

One of our librarians joins in at various junctures and contributes to and benefits from the group's expertise. The Reading Ninjas have permission to purchase books on behalf of the library at local bookstores and via our online OverDrive and Follett accounts.

If you decide to have a go at forming your own Reading Ninjas club, check out the "Toolkit" below for ideas.

TOOLKIT FOR NINJAS

See page 269 for links.

See page 269 for links.

- "25 Ideas to Motivate Readers": Good ideas from teachers
- Arts & Letters Daily: A simply amazing array of literature, trends, etc.
- Fandom: Passionate fans of books and other media
- Google Books Ngram Viewer: Charts the frequency of searches on Google for any word during a given period of time
- Library Book Face's Photos: Helpful for promoting reading
- TheNounProject.com: Find an icon for everything
- PrintWhatYouLike.com: Type in a URL and then cut, paste, and print
- Readers' Advisory for Youth: Matches readers with books
- Reading Ladders: Helps readers to progress from easy to more challenging reading
- Reading Promotion Ideas: Pinterest board with good ideas for marketing books
- TodaysMeet: Chat during a movie to keep viewers engaged

OUR RAISON D'ÊTRE

Let's try a quick word association test. If I say "libraries," what is the first word that comes to mind? Is it "learning," "exploration," "discovery," "collaboration," "facilitation," "access," "research," "creation," or "inspiration"? No, it's most likely "books." I'm no different than you—it's like a reflex. Books dominate libraries, and books are a treasure that libraries share with glee. I love books, stories, and the amazing way they can transport me to a far larger universe than my mind alone is capable. As a librarian, I have been incredibly fortunate to have had the opportunity to meet and get to know some amazing writers, storytellers, historians, poets, and adventurers whom we call authors, including Chris Crutcher, Steve Sheinkin, Candace Fleming, Ying Compestine, and Linda Sue Park. I've come to admire all these authors even more as I struggle to write this book.

Despite all of this, books may not be libraries' focal point in the future. Yes, I know this is blasphemy and runs counter to the arguments put forth by author and reading advocate Neil Gaiman in the first chapter, but you must understand I am not against books—I am simply wanting our libraries to support, encourage, and facilitate all forms of learning for all types of learners. Books will always play an important part in this learning, but they do not have to be in print form, nor should they be restricted from having media content. Historically, libraries, and especially the ALA, have supported this kind of access to information, "regardless of technology, format, or methods of delivery."

The diversity and forms of digital and non-digital media are growing, and we must embrace all of the informational formats that best serve our patrons' needs. We must continue investigating the new disciplines, apps, techniques, knowledge bases, instruments, and tools for learning we have at our disposal. We cannot afford to simply restrict ourselves to books or printed literature—we need to make greater efforts to provide our members with the full spectrum of resources to address the problems and challenges they'll be facing in this century. After all, lifelong learning is our *raison d'être*, our very reason for existence, and lifelong learning occurs across all settings, through all forms, and with all types of intelligence. We must avoid being book snobs and embrace gaming, music, the arts, engineering, dance, sports, and entertainment if we really want to fully embrace learning.

CHAPTER 15

Counting on Logic

Logic is the beginning of wisdom, not the end.
—*Spock,* Star Trek VI: The Undiscovered Country

The old television series *Star Trek* **had a popular first officer** called Mr. Spock who was half Vulcan and half human. Vulcans are known for their dispassionate use of logic and reasoning, so Spock makes a good candidate to serve as our avatar for logical mathematical intelligence.

Spock: "It is only logical that you should select a Vulcan to introduce you to logical/mathematical intelligence. Insufficient facts always invite danger. This 'center for design', as you call it, allows you to test your ideas and separate fact from fiction."

LOGICAL/MATHEMATICAL INTELLIGENCE

When was the last time a math or a science class came into your library? The psychology and education fields have shown a strong preference for linguistic and logical/mathematical intelligences, and both of these intelligences appear to have a strong connection to general intelligence. However, traditional libraries devote considerable attention to linguistic intelligence, while devoting very little to the logical/mathematical side.

In Gardner's multiple intelligences theory, logical/mathematical intelligence involves more than math; it employs reasoning and critical thinking and focuses on the ability to see patterns, sequences, puzzles, numerical relationships, abstractions, and number relationships. Scientific investigation and deductive reasoning embrace this type of intelligence.

CENTER FOR DESIGN

Design Center at SAS

I think I can best illustrate logical/mathematical intelligence using a recent project from our design center. One of our school's science teachers asked if we could help his students in constructing "pop pop boats" out of pop cans and milk cartons. The project involved measurement, following instructions, arranging patterns, and deductive reasoning. Over the course of two class periods, each student built a working boat, and in the end, they learned about the physics behind heat, pressure, motion, and expansion. Overall, the students seemed to enjoy the process, and though they were pressed for time, they did gain hands-on experience with problem solving, designing, and small-scale engineering.

Projects such as this one engage students in practicing several forms of intelligence, and if done properly, they can instill a greater sense of confidence as well as a much deeper understanding of the physics principles involved.

Unfortunately, due to a number of constraints, including time and resources, classroom teachers are often forced to mass-produce one type of project. In this case, the teacher had five classes of twenty-five students each, meaning he needed the materials, tools, and space to produce more than a hundred pop pop boats! Ideally, every student would have been able to design and build a unique project, but one-size-fits-all projects are sometimes necessary to allow a standardized assessment of skills and ensure common learning. However, libraries with maker spaces or centers for design have more flexibility to individualize projects, since students can store their work and come back to it during breaks or before or after school.

We rarely rely on just one type of intelligence to accomplish everyday tasks in life, so in our library, we use the multiple intelligences theory to ensure we're supporting all types of learning. It helps us see if we are missing anything. We begin to look for any gaps and areas in need of support when we ask ourselves, "Have we included tools, materials, and space to accommodate each intelligence?" In traditional g factor models of intelligence, problem solving involving musical, spatial, or interpersonal and intrapersonal intelligence is often neglected. So when students view 3-D images of cell biology on our library's Oculus Rift or zSpace and then identify relationships between multiple things, they're engaging in many types of intelligence, including logical/mathematical and spatial intelligence.

TOOLKIT FOR LOGICAL / MATHEMATICAL INTELLIGENCE
See page 270 for links.

- AWW: A white board app that allows you to draw or do math

- Chibitronics: Kits with templates to teach basic electronics

- The Curiosity Box: Science experiments

- GeoGebra: Offers a wide variety of geometric examples and visual aids

- LittleBits: Tiny electronic building blocks

- Scratch: Allows you to program your own games and animations

- Thingiverse: For use with 3-D printing

- Tickle: Uses coding to control Sphero, drones, and other devices

- Tinkercad: Allows for 3-D design and printing

- Wolfram Alpha: A search engine for mathematical applications

LET THE GAMES BEGIN

Libraries offer math and science resources, yet they rarely incorporate science or math displays, let alone hands-on math, science, or logic opportunities. Enter online gaming, one of the easiest ways to draw on logical/mathematical intelligence. The gaming movement is growing incredibly fast, engaging students of all ages.

Our eighth-grade math students designed a game involving the math principles of probability and chance. They brought their games into the library for a "Math Games Fair," took turns playing each other's games, and sharing the mathematical principles behind their work.

AN HOUR OF CODE

Our library's Hour of Code workshops engage students in another growth area that uses logical/mathematical intelligence: coding. These one-hour workshops teach newcomers and more experienced students alike how to program in a fun, accessible way.

I was initially apprehensive when I joined the group of middle school students for my first Hour of Code—I don't necessarily love computer workshops and prefer learning computer skills one-on-one, so I can go at my own slow pace. But I was pleasantly surprised that the Hour of Code took me through a gentle progression that I could follow. I was able to complete the tasks and felt a sense of accomplishment when my LEGO figure moved according to plan. Each year, over 164,000 Hour of Code events are held around the world. "The Hour of Code is driven by the Hour of Code and Computer Science Education Week Advisory and Review Committees as well as an unprecedented coalition of partners..."

After hosting an online Hour of Code at our school, we invited students with experience in coding to participate in a Sphero obstacle course.

Many schools have established their own Hour of Code programs, and students are working on all sorts of creative projects. If you'd like to start your own Hour of Code, "Toolkit" below includes a few resources to help.

TOOLKIT FOR HOUR OF CODE
See page 271 for links.

- Angry Birds with Code: Allows students to move around the Angry Birds.

- Coding with Scratch: Allows students to create animations with coding and scratch.

- "How to Teach One Hour of Code": Provides instructions on how to conduct specific Hour of Code lessons.

APPY HOUR

When I got my first iPhone, I fell in love with the apps. Like many other people, I went crazy downloading apps that I didn't have any time to use. And after a couple of years, I had so many on my phone that I was overwhelmed and only used a few. I needed to weed my app library. I knew I wanted to stay current on the most useful and entertaining apps, so I decided to crowdsource the best ones by hosting an "Appy Hour" in the library. It was amazing how many new apps we all learned about. In fact, we were overwhelmed with too many choices and not enough time, but it was fun and well received.

Here's how an Appy Hour works:

1. Decide if you'll focus on apps for iOS (Apple) or Android.
2. Browse the app store and determine the five to ten categories that would be most relevant to the people attending your event.

3. Choose one or two of your favorite apps for each category to get the ball rolling.

4. Advertise the event and offer a few snacks (if you can).

5. Introduce your first category and ask for suggestions. Each person must step up to the mic and describe their favorite app for this category in sixty seconds or less.

6. Add the app's name and link to a Google Doc to share with the audience after the event.

A Night (or Day) at the Museum

Science museums are wonderful examples of highly supportive learning environments for logical/mathematical intelligence, and I've found they typically offer great hands-on activities that can trigger ideas for our own libraries. So if you have a museum of science and industry or the equivalent near you, take a field trip and bring along some of your library's members, if possible, so you can get their input for your library.

Small Is Beautiful

When you begin considering how your learning design studio or zone will support students' logical/mathematical intelligence, remember, you can start at a very low cost. Each time your library launches a new project or service, market the feature by creating a short, thirty- to sixty-second video explaining it. You may consider making a longer one, but I suggest starting with a minute or less and then making a second one no longer than three minutes, if needed, to explain the concept or activity.

Artistic Puzzles

Origami is, of course, a fantastic activity for logical/mathematical thinking and spatial awareness, and the Internet is home to countless free designs that challenge students to make both simple and complex creations, like the ones shown below.

Math teachers and students need our help in showing how math relates to the real world. How many times have students asked, "When will we ever use this?" They deserve a proper answer, and one way to demonstrate real-life applications of math is through hands-on projects. The tools I offer in the "Toolkit for Logical Stuff" are simply a starting point.

Math can be found in everything we do. Pointing this out to students as they work on their projects can make math come alive.

TOOLKIT FOR LOGICAL STUFF

See page 271 for links.

- Abacus: How to use a Chinese abacus
- Chess: Physical or digital
- Checkers: Try Western or Chinese
- Curriki: Free learning resources for students from kindergarten through college
- Khan Academy: Excellent math tutorials
- Paper models: Perfect for beginners
- Quantified Self: Track your habits
- String art patterns: Thirty-five DIY patterns
- WikiHow: Drawing parabolic curves with straight lines

CHAPTER 16

A Sound Perspective

Music expresses that which cannot be put into words and that which cannot remain silent.

—*Victor Hugo*

When we say "musical intelligence," we're talking about a person's sensitivity and ability to follow a rhythm or hear the difference between a flat note and a sharp one. A person possessing good musical intelligence might be able to easily pick out a song's melody, identify the instruments in a symphony performance, have good pitch, be able to sing, easily learn a new instrument, or compose a song. This intelligence helps us grasp chord progressions, tonality, harmonies, pitch, and tempo and plays a role in our receptiveness to auditory learning and instruction.

In *Frames of Mind*, author Gardner writes:

> *Individuals may make their initial encounter with music through different media and modalities and, even more so, continue to encounter music in idiosyncratic fashion. Thus, while every normal individual is exposed to natural language primarily through listening to others speak, humans can encounter music through many channels: singing, playing instruments by hand, inserting instruments into the mouth, reading of musical notation, listening to records, watching dances, or the like.*

Listening to music in a library setting can work—with the right selections. In our library, we have a quiet side and a collaborative side with a glass wall separating the two. Although we've opted to keep the quiet side music-free, on the collaborative side, we play mood music from Spotify. We've chosen playlists with names like "Acoustic Covers," "House Relax," "Afternoon Acoustic," and "Your Favorite Coffee House," as we've found music with lyrics or too much energy can be distracting or disruptive. We have been playing music on our collaborative side of the library for the last four years and have yet to receive a complaint from any of our library members. We tend to play a wide range of music including folk guitar, soft jazz, classical, electronic, or country. We do play pop, rock, and other genres with lyrics when we are staging more active events in the library.

THE NOTEPAD

Overlooking the harbor at the National Library Board's (NLB) library@esplanade in Singapore is an all-glass room with a baby grand piano. The room is partially soundproof, and library members may book it for practice and enjoyment. These gentle rehearsals create soft background music for library patrons sitting in the nearby reading area. This same performing arts library also has a music performance studio equipped with electric guitars, a digital drum set, and numerous other instruments. This is a public library that has made a conscious effort to support musical intelligence by facilitating musical content creation.

Ben Robertoccio in the "Notepad"

You may be thinking, "We don't have the budget for that sort of thing, and I don't have time to teach music, nor do I even know how to play an instrument. My boss would have a fit if I tried to do that in the library I work in." Trust me, I had the same thoughts, but seeing the music studio in the NLB's library gave me the confidence I needed that I had the library profession's permission to go forward.

We started small by taking my former office and putting in a few pieces of equipment loaned to us by the music department, just to test the waters. We didn't spend a lot of money, but we tried to figure out what would spark students' interest. Students were amazed and excited by the fact that we would even consider allowing them to play musical instruments in the library. We were encouraged to slowly add new instruments and features to the room.

We felt the best way to market the studio would be to name it "Notepad" and make a video showing how it works. The video tells the story of a new student (played by our assistant superintendent, who happens to love music) being introduced to the studio.[1] Our music teachers got involved and transformed "Pachelbel's Canon in D" from classical to rock.

The Notepad is a fully equipped recording studio designed for play. We want experienced musicians and audio-recording buffs, as well as first-time musicians and recorders to use this studio. We encourage students to try new instruments and record their experiments with sound and music. The Notepad is also the perfect place to work on classroom projects or gain inspiration from a world of auditory possibilities.

The studio has minimal acoustic paneling (we ran short of funds), so we usually ask students to use headphones, unless the library is empty. In that case, they can switch to the external speakers. Most of the studio's instruments are digital, so students can easily record their tracks using GarageBand or Logic Pro. The studio can support a rock band or a four-string quartet using headphones and merging their sounds through a device known as "Apogee." The one thing we wish we had done differently is design the studio to better accommodate the needs of our younger population, but we are working on this.

To illustrate our audio studio's features and demonstrate musical intelligence, our library's staff created an avatar named "Mrs. Crabshaw," the stereotypical cranky librarian, who morphs into a cool dude named Jacob. Jacob describes the studio's instruments and offers students musical possibilities to explore. Our hope is that by having the avatar describe the space's features, the students find the content more interesting and less threatening than if it were coming from an adult. Once a student listens to the characters' presentation, one of our staff members follows up to answer any questions they may have.

---

1   Watch the video here: bit.ly/2ipWFbg

Mrs. Crabshaw: "Well, it's about time you came in here. My name is Mrs. Crabshaw, and I'll have you know I don't expect any nonsense in here. Now, sit down and listen carefully while I tell you what this recording studio is all about. And shush—I want it so quiet in here that I can hear a pin drop.

"What? You don't want to stay? You don't feel comfortable around me?"

Jacob: "Okay, I can see you are cool. I just needed to use the Crabshaw cover in case some teacher or librarian thought you might be having fun. My name is Jacob, and this is going to be very cool.

"Dude, I gotta tell you—this little room you have just entered is awesome. In the private studio, you can rehearse or record lead guitar, bass guitar, digital drums, string quartet, vocals, and a wide range of other instruments. You can produce podcasts, record audio books, or remix or compose your own sounds."

To create our avatars, my staff and I use animation software called "CrazyTalk." I like this program, because unlike our earlier renditions, CrazyTalk allows you to create avatars that can walk and move about. Plus, it's perfect for beginners. If you'd prefer a more sophisticated avatar, a simple Google search will show you the many other programs available.

How Does Musical Acoustic Intelligence Sound?

Our acoustic world is incredibly vast. Listen to Spotify, Pandora, or iHeartRadio for just a few minutes to hear a sampling of the variety of music being created. Play a podcast and listen to some of the planet's greatest minds speak to you in their own voices, complete with human emotions, inflections, and passion. Go outside and listen to the dogs barking, birds chirping, or cars racing by; we live in a world of sounds, and to a great extent, we interpret these sounds through our musical acoustic intelligence.

Schools generally teach classical music designed for bands and orchestras. I learned to play the trumpet in high school, and I fully enjoyed it, but I know it isn't for everyone. (I later played the euphonium just for fun in a Swiss Oktoberfest band.) I would've loved to have played guitar or piano, but they weren't options in my school, nor are they options in most schools.

Restricting music education to string instruments (violins, cellos, and violas), brass instruments, (trumpets, trombones, and French horns), and woodwinds (clarinets or oboes) has worked well for centuries from an organizational standpoint, as you can place a single music teacher in a room with fifty or more music students and accommodate a wide range of instruments. This approach works well for some jazz, classical music, and big band music, but it doesn't work well for rock, folk, country, and electronic music, nor does it work well for students who are interested in playing instruments such as the guitar or piano.

Although my middle- and high school musical education helped develop my appreciation for classical music, like the majority of students and listening audiences, I spend most of my time listening to contemporary music, which traditional music education largely ignores.

In "Why Music Lessons Need to Keep up with the Times," Clint Randles, PhD, an associate professor of music education at the University of South Florida, suggests music teachers should function as music producers by helping students make their own music. "I believe music classes today should teach students to create, record, and share their music that comes from their personal interests." Having a music studio like the "Notepad" allows more personalization of music education and draws in students who might not have the courage to attempt booking a music studio in the music department. Even with a modest setup, you can facilitate musical content creation and generate an interest in music with students who may have never considered taking a music class or learning how to play an instrument. If you're curious about the equipment we've collected over the years, "Music Studio Toolkit" on page 150 lists our current inventory.

I'm not trying to promote these products; they are simply a list of the equipment we use in our library music studio. You don't need all this equipment to get started. All you really need is a laptop computer with software such as Garage Band to do recording and one or two digital instruments such as the midi piano keyboard, a guitar, a set of headphones and a good microphone you can plug into a laptop or iPad. You can build from there.

Build Your Own Symphony

With a little creativity, libraries can support their students' musical intelligence in a number of fun ways. If your music studio is set up to be plug-and-play, you might find some students trying new instruments. With digital instruments, students without any prior musical experience can try a guitar, drums, or keyboard while listening to their musical masterpieces through their headphones. As they gain confidence, they may even try their recording skills or perhaps jam with friends.

When you start crossing intelligences, you can come up with some very creative forms of learning. For example, James, our consultant, decided to build a hobo guitar in our design center using a cigar box and parts from a discarded guitar. When he discovered cigar boxes are a rare commodity in Singapore, he used a cookie tin instead. In "The 3-Stringed Hobo Guitar by SAS MS Library,"[2] filmed by our colleague Shahrin Aripin, you can see and hear the incredible quality of sound James was able to produce using a very simple design. He was simply

2   Watch the video here: http://bit.ly/2hhTl3Y

MUSIC STUDIO TOOLKIT

- 2 External speakers (M-Audio BX5)
- 1 External microphone (Se X1)
- 1 Pop filter to reduce distortion on voice recordings (vc m2 pcs)
- 1 Microphone (Apogee)
- 1 Digital drum kit (Yamaha DTX450K)
- 2 Locking guitar stands
- 1 Vintage bass guitar (SX)
- 1 Maple lead guitar (ESP LTD ST-213)
- 1 Ukulele (Kahua 24B OC)
- 1 Audio interface for iPad and Mac (Apogee Quartet)
- 2 Audio interface mics for Mac (Apogee ONE)
- 1 JamHub BedRoom Silent Rehearsal Studio
- 1 MIDI controller (M-Audio Keystation Mini 32 Ultra-Portable 32-Key USB MIDI Keyboard Controller)
- 1 Electric violin (Ted Brewer Vivo2)
- 2 Mini-keyboards (Akai Professional MPK Mini 25-Key Ultra-Portable USB MIDI Keyboard Controller)
- 1 MIDI controller (M-Audio AXIOM 49 Advanced 49-Key Semi-Weighted USB MIDI controller)
- 1 Condenser microphone (MXL GENESIS FET Premium Large-D)

MUSIC STUDIO TOOLKIT (CONT.)

- 3 Closed-back monitoring headphones (Shure SRH240A)
- 3 Semi-open tracking headphones (PreSonus HD7 Professional)
- 1 Vocal isolation screen with stand (SM Pro Audio Mic Thing)
- 1 Cello (NS Design NXTa 5-String Cello with Amber Burst)
- 1 Viola (NS Design CR4 4-String Electric Viola, Amber)

throwing out bait to our preteen audience who come into the library to discover things in the company of friends.

By helping students to build their own instruments, they take much greater pride in the instrument and the music they are creating, they learn more about how the musical notes are produced, and how you can then alter the sounds using the instrument and player. Now James has a growing cadre of students hunting down cookie tins and cigar boxes so they, too, can build their own instruments. In this process, students are utilizing mathematical logical intelligence, body kinesthetic intelligence, and musical acoustic intelligence.

TOOLKIT FOR
MUSIC AND SOUND

See page 272 for links.

- 28 Records: Use your laptop keys to produce twenty-eight sounds.

- Arpeggios: Select from a wheel of combinations for each music arrangement.

- Booktrack Classroom: Write a story and add sound effects.

- Cassette Tape: Add hip-hop beats along with your own voice.

- Chords: Lets you see and hear each major and minor chord.

- Chrome Music Lab: Produce different sound and music experiments.

- Free Music Archive: Use royalty-free music.

- Free Soundtrack Music: Find more royalty-free music.

- Harmonics: Use six visuals that work like tuning forks.

- Jamendo Music: Expand your choices for royalty-free music.

- Kandinsky: Produce notes through drawing.

- Melody Maker: Create visual melodies.

- Oscillators: Listen and alter different oscillation types and frequencies.

- Piano Roll: Use it for its old player piano functions.

- Rhythm: Create different rhythms with animated percussion.

- Soundtrap.com

TOOLKIT FOR MUSIC AND SOUND (CONT.)

- Sound Waves: See and hear the soundwave each note produces.

- Spectrogram: Visualize your voice or instrument's wavelengths.

- Strings: Explore the relationship between string length and pitch.

- Theremin: Experiment with sounds through delay, feedback, and scuzz.

- Voice Spinner: Use different speeds to alter sounds.

- UJam: Hum a tune and then convert it into an instrument.

Source: chromeexperiments.com

Chapter 17

Just Picture It

Art enables us to find ourselves and lose ourselves at the same time.

—Thomas Merton, No Man Is an Island

W hat could a sculptor and an airline pilot possibly have in common? Well, for one, they both use spatial intelligence to create mental maps and a visual memory of the spaces they're operating in. Whereas the sculptor may use a person or simply their imagination to create a 3-D object out of clay, wood, marble, or another medium, the pilot uses her experiences to create mental and digital maps and visual observations to navigate and make judgments about the physical space her plane is passing through.

Spatial intelligence allows us to notice fine details, patterns, color variations, textures, and changes and helps us see the spatial relationships necessary for drawing, painting, reading maps, and even daydreaming. For these reasons, we sometimes refer to spatial intelligence as "visual intelligence" or "artistic intelligence," since they all involve visualizing objects, people, and places from many angles and points of view.

Individuals with a high aptitude in spatial intelligence tend to think in three-dimensional terms and be visual learners, meaning they best grasp information when it's presented as maps, charts, graphs, and infographics. They can remember visual images and then adapt and modify them using mental maps. These visual learners often do well creating art, decorating, designing architecture, conceiving designs, working with objects, using eye-hand coordination, and solving problems that involve spatial judgments.

Your spatial judgment and ability to visualize with your mind's eye are enhanced by creating videos, digital pictures, and artistic creations, so we created a visual capture studio (the "Tiger's Eye") and dedicated it to exploring visual media projects. At any one time, up to five students can be in the studio experimenting with the cameras and other equipment, creating videos and taking photos for class projects or simply for fun.

The Tiger's Eye: A Photography and Videography Studio

We installed green, white, and black pull-down screens, but you could accomplish the same effect by simply painting the walls green. (Green screens provide a solid backdrop color, which is, hopefully, different from the clothing or items you're filming or photographing. Later on, in the editing phase, you can replace the green background with the color or scene of your choice.) Since we built the facility, students have been booking it quite often.

As with other areas of the library, Mr. T, the avatar mascot, is there to introduce students to the studio. In the video titled "The Koltutsky Tiger,"[1] you can listen to Mr. T talking about connections.

---

1   Watch the video here: bit.ly/2hlRYOA

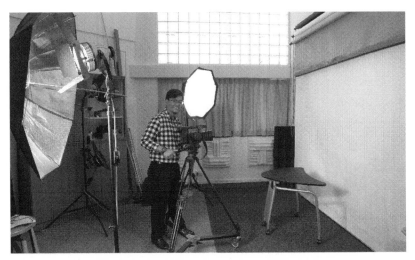

Shahrin Aripin, our maker and creation studio technician

The Koltutsky Tiger, the avatar mascot of the Tiger's Eye

LEARNING THROUGH SPATIAL INTELLIGENCE

In subtle and not-so-subtle ways, schools often convey the message to students that certain types of intelligence and subjects like art and music are not true measures of intellect and are, therefore, less important. For example, artists are cool and innovative, but these students are sometimes seen as less intelligent or hardworking than, say, science or math students. However, Daniel Pink argues in *A Whole New Mind* that changes in our society are making subjects, such as art and design, more highly valued. I could go on at great length about the creative genius of artists, photographers, musicians, and sculptors, but I think you get the picture. As "new librarians," we have an obligation to support all forms of intelligence, not simply the three R's.

I CAN PICTURE THAT

Libraries and art galleries form a perfect marriage, and local art displayed within the library creates a feeling of community. While the books draw the library members to the art, the art draws the artists to the books. Photographic displays can create a new sense of wonder, new perspectives, new thoughts, and new connections across the community and disciplines. (And, of course, book displays positioned alongside artwork is a perfect blend.) So school, academic, and public library librarians should make an effort to forge partnerships with local artists and art teachers.

SPANISH WEATHER REPORTS

My school's Spanish teachers came up with the idea of filming their students presenting weather reports in Spanish, resulting in an obvious combination of linguistic and spatial intelligence. Using the green screen in the Tiger's Eye, we added an image of a TV studio in the background, creating a realistic appearance. The students and parents all loved the completed videos.

TOOLKIT FOR
VISUAL / SPATIAL INTELLIGENCE
See page 274 for links.

- 3-D City: Is a 3-D city builder
- Canva: Creates a design for infographics
- Copainter: Allows you to collaborate on drawings.
- Google Cardboard: Provides an inexpensive VR for any smartphone
- Gush: Allows you to produce interactive art
- House Configurator: Allows you to build houses you can visit in 3-D
- Internet Graffiti Board: Is a digital bulletin board
- Just A Reflektor: Is an interactive video
- 3D Lego Designer: Allows you to build with 3-D LEGOs
- motionEmotion: Provides emotion and gesture-based art form
- Oimo.js: Is a 3-D physics application
- Quietube: Provides YouTube without distractions
- SceneJS: Allows you to see architectural flybys
- SculptGL: Allows you to do digital sculpting
- Slides Carnival: Offers templates for Google Slides presentations
- Stop Motion Studio: Is a video-production app
- TubeChop: Allows you to take a portion of a YouTube video
- Video Notes: Allows you to comment on YouTube videos

DIGITAL ART

Outside of our photo studio, we've incorporated additional equipment to facilitate students' spatial intelligence through digital art, including iPads, Wacom, and Bamboo art tablets. A variety of digital art programs, some free and some expensive, are available online for these devices. We also have a large-scale printer, allowing us to scan artwork and create infographics and posters for classes and clubs.

MARKETING THE IDEA

Projecting digital art and photography onto large screens or using LED monitors can add a fun, new dynamic to any library. And when you add music and art (even from beginning artists) to the projections, the library's entrance experience can easily transform from dull to dramatic.

The promise of a Wacom tablet is one surefire way to lure artists into your library, where they can then produce works of art for your members' enjoyment. There's great value in allowing students who have never taken an art class to view the artistic process as it unfolds. You may also encourage your school's art teachers to bring their art classes into the library to work alongside students working on other types of projects.

IT'S EASY TO GET STARTED

Creating a beginning photography studio is far easier than creating an audio studio—all you need is a digital device with a camera. And while a dedicated digital camera, tripod to mount the camera on, and good lighting all certainly make a big difference, they aren't essential to start. You can also create a green or blue screen on the cheap by painting a wall or even hanging a color sheet.

Plus, digital photography is easy to archive and display on the library's LED screens, increasing the environment's appeal while showcasing student work and stimulating and drawing patrons' attention to spatial intelligence.

TOOLKIT FOR A
PHOTOGRAPHY / VIDEOGRAPHY STUDIO

- Bamboo slate: A digital drawing pad

- DSLR camera: A Digital Single-Lens Reflex camera

- Equipment cabinet: To store and protect equipment

- Large-format printer: To create large posters from photographs or artwork

- Photography lamps: To control the lighting in the studio

- Scanner: To digitize artwork for later production

- Tripods: For the cameras and videocams

- Video camera: Standalone or built into a DSLR camera

- Visualizer: For projecting artwork onto a large screen

- Wacom tablet: An artist's digital tablet

CHAPTER 18

Let's Get Physical

*What you do and learn in life physically changes what your
brain looks like—it literally rewires it.*

—*John Medina,* Brain Rules

When I need inspiration for my library, sometimes I will visit shopping malls. They market themselves well and make their spaces visually appealing, and I've found they're often more innovative than libraries. While on one such excursion, I noticed several exercise bikes like the ones pictured in on the next page. I liked the bikes' design and thought they might work well in the library.

Middle school students (ages eleven through thirteen) are built to move and fidget. It kills them to sit in classes all day with few opportunities to stand up, walk around, and move. With this in mind, I avoided asking permission and simply introduced one exercise bike into the library. I waited for pushback from teachers, or worse yet, the principal. I waited for trouble to erupt with students horsing around. I waited with a prepared speech for parents with complaints. None of that happened.

The Wellness Zone for kinesthetic intelligence

People were intrigued. They wanted to try the bike out, and they all asked if we required people to read while they were on it. We don't require patrons to read while cycling, but it's certainly an option. Our goal is to get people moving, because by moving, they can better focus on their reading and assignments and remember what they're learning.

We eventually acquired a few more pieces of equipment, including a large treadmill and an even larger StairMaster®. The students loved them, but over time, we found it much easier to maintain and repair less-complicated items with fewer moving parts.

The more we read about the connections between exercise and learning, the more our Wellness Zone just made sense. In fact, Illinois' Naperville Central High School structures its entire school around daily exercise, so we thought we could try out the concept on a much smaller scale.

And so the "Wellness Zone" was officially born. As you can see in the photo on the previous page, it's not large and we didn't displace any books, but nevertheless, it is a popular and well-used area that gets students moving and promotes wellness.

Middle school students are made to squirm—it's in their very nature. Watch a classroom where the teacher insists on lecturing preteens for longer than thirty minutes, and you'll see a classroom with students fidgeting, talking if they can get away with it, and moving in whichever way possible. If these students could get up and move around, they would actually focus, think, and remember more.

The possibilities for facilitating bodily-kinesthetic intelligence within your library are endless. You could create a calories photo board encouraging healthier eating, or even include a juice bar, if you have the space and volunteers to run it.

KINESTHETIC INTELLIGENCE

We all appreciate the incredible timing, balance, and grace that expert dancers exhibit. We recognize gymnasts' strength, agility, flexibility, and talent. We are amazed by the virtuoso performances of pianists, guitarists, and other musicians whose art requires expert timing, dexterity, and coordination. And we can see the complexity involved in motor racing, archery, and even magic performances. Yet, we rarely think of these fine and gross motor activities as intelligence.

Gardner and his colleagues have been studying the complex sequences of physical actions performed by athletes, musicians, actors, and other performers for decades. In *Frames of Mind,* he says,

> *This divorce between the mental and the physical has not infrequently been coupled with a notion that what we do with our bodies is somewhat less privileged, less special, than those problem-solving routines carried out chiefly through the use of language, logic, or some other relatively abstract symbolic system.*

Gardner describes these highly skilled and balanced movements that allow the human body to achieve extraordinary feats as "bodily-kinesthetic intelligence." A superb sense of timing, complex eye-hand coordination, exquisite, and graceful movements along with balance, rhythm, agility, speed, and flexibility are all characteristics of this intelligence.

According to Gardner, "It is just because of this mastery of the possible alternatives, the ability to enact the sequence most effective for present purposes, that the expert looks as though he has all the time in the world to do what he wants."

Middle school students in our library love our wellness area. In the two years we've had the Wellness Zone, it has been a huge success. It's popular with students and parents alike, and teachers say they can see a difference in the students who were pulled away from computer screens during their breaks.

In "Why Not Even Exercise Will Undo the Harm of Sitting All Day—And What You Can Do About It," health journalist Hannah Newman points to research published in *The American Journal of Clinical Nutrition*, showing that a person's glucose metabolism can improve with just one minute and forty seconds of walking every thirty minutes for every nine hours spent sitting, while the American Diabetes Association recommends that for every five hours, we should do two minutes of light-intensity walking on a treadmill every twenty minutes.

Researchers at the University of Regensburg in Germany and the Sax Institute in Australia found sitting for prolonged periods of time can lead to the ailments below:

- Increases in several types of cancer
- Decreases in the bodily electrical activity needed to create beneficial molecules
- Increased obesity

- Decreases in lipoprotein lipase, an enzyme that vacuums up fat in the blood stream
- The suppression of a gene that supports the cardiovascular system by controlling inflammation and blood clotting
- Shortened lifespan

In contrast, the anticipated benefits of regular physical activity include the following:

- Improving your focus and attention
- Improving your memory and brain power
- Increasing your self-confidence and self-esteem
- Managing your energy, anger, and pain
- Improving your happiness quotient
- Managing your stress and your ability to relax

John Ratey, MD, wrote the book *Spark: The Revolutionary New Science of Exercise and the Brain*, which documents the effectiveness of the Napierville Central High School program, along with other studies of the effects of exercise on cognitive abilities and academic performance, as well as improvements in emotional health.

"OKAY, I SORTA GET IT"

Exercise is good for you, but why have a Wellness Zone in a library? Think about it: What better place to get people's attention and drive the point home that we sit far too much? Helping your library members learn about wellness and engaging them in facilitating their bodily-kinesthetic intelligence is all part of the library of the future's efforts to improve society and add to knowledge creation.

Getting started is easy—simply purchase a simple step machine, standing desk, or bicycle machine that only occupies a small amount of floor space and watch what happens. If members are afraid to use one lone device, put up a sign letting them know it is okay, along with a list featuring some of the health benefits. If the idea appeals to your library members, ask them what other devices they would like to see in your growing Wellness Zone.

Team up with Your P.E. Department

Naperville Central High School in Naperville, Illinois, decided to do their own action research on the effects of exercise within the academic achievement, and the results have been dramatic. The Illinois Public Health Institute reported in 2013 that requiring students to exercise daily within targeted heart rate zones has led to huge improvements in the school's reading and math scores.

To see if your school can achieve similar results, team up with your P.E. department, and perhaps they'll give you a few pieces of equipment to start. Books on fitness and nutrition should certainly play a part in your overall setup, as should posters and some basic instructions.

Stand Up

Studies conducted in America, Australia, and Europe are showing the damaging effects of too much sitting. By working at a standing desk for just a few minutes throughout the day, you improve your health and increase your longevity. In 2016, The Los Angeles Times reported new research is finding that those people who sit for long periods of time raise their average risk of Type 2 diabetes, early death, cardiovascular disease, and cancer.

Neurofeedback and Biometrics

FitBit, Jawbone, and Garmin's personal biometric devices are simpler versions of more sophisticated biofeedback (aka neurofeedback) equipment. They're offering everyday people feedback on their heart rate, muscle response, and galvanic skin response, and as a result, these individuals are learning how to reduce stress and more efficiently promote healthy practices in their daily lives. Heart rate, blood pressure, and BMI are key variables in maintaining good health. Regulating one's stress is also essential.

By establishing a Wellness Zone, libraries can provide the space, the tools, and the training students and faculty need to become healthier, more efficient learners.

Brain Rules

In 2016, developmental molecular biologist John Medina, PhD, visited SAS Middle School and did his well-known "Brain Rules" talks, explaining how exercise helps the brain function by improving concentration, impulse control, foresight, and problem solving. During his walk-through, Medina gave us a positive thumbs-up for our library's efforts in the Wellness Zone, reaffirming that we're on the right track in supporting our students' wellness. Since his visit, we've made his "Brain Rules" YouTube videos easily accessible to students in the Wellness Zone using a stationary iPad equipped with headphones. A couple of my favorite Brain Rules are *Brain Rule 1: Exercise Boosts Brain Power* (watch Medina's video here: bit.ly/2hbKjTa) and *Brain Rule 8: Stressed Brains Don't Learn as Effectively* (bit.ly/2hT5FbA).

Other studies' findings are supporting Medina's work. *New York Times'* writer Gretchen Reynolds cites research from the National Institutes of Health pointing to a protein called "cathepsin B," a protein the body produces during exercise, which then significantly improved the memory and thinking of study participants.

The research is clear and the solution is simple: As twenty-first-century librarians, we should encourage our patrons to exercise more so they can think more clearly and live healthier, happier lives. Adding a Wellness Zone to your library is a step in the right direction.

CHAPTER 19

Listening to Mother Nature

You didn't come into this world, you came out of it, like a
wave from the ocean. You are not a stranger here.

—Alan Watts

W
e can facilitate naturalistic intelligence in our libraries by showcasing objects from the natural world, having signage about endangered species, showing how to collect data, displaying plant and insect collections, featuring books about nature, and recognizing the work of famous naturalists, such as John Muir, Rachel Carson, Charles Darwin, George Washington Carver, and Luther Burbank.

Visits to sites such as natural history museums, botanical gardens, zoos, farms, centers for oceanography and marine biology, planetariums, agricultural research centers, and nature reserves can enhance your own naturalistic intelligence and spark amazing ideas for promoting naturalistic understanding and awareness.

To create an area dedicated to naturalistic intelligence, my staff and I transformed a rather dark, closed-in room that served as a book processing and cataloging area into an open space called the "Living Room." Eventually, we plan to install an aquarium with a terrarium inside (an invention originally designed by Dave Butcher, a friend of mine in college), as well as a large glass-enclosed ant farm so students can learn about biologist E.O. Wilson's work and make discoveries of their own in the fields of myrmecology and sociobiology.

We've designed the Living Room to look like a real living room, complete with deep, comfy chairs and a serene, quiet environment. Books about science, nature, and climate change are housed here, and plants, animals, and visual displays showing infographics on global climate change emphasize a more naturalistic look.

We have made climate change a central feature of our "Living Room" area since it impacts our view of nature locally and globally. By focusing on this huge social and environmental issue, we are staying true to our library mission statement and the mission advocated for librarians by David Lankes in his book *The Atlas of New Librarianship:* "The mission of librarians is to improve society through facilitating knowledge creation in their communities."

Climate change will force us to think much more about nature in the coming decades, resulting in a chain of side effects that will require major changes in how we produce and use energy, protect endangered species and endangered environments, and create sustainable practices that don't contribute to our carbon footprint or deplete our natural resources. In pressing this issue, we are promoting naturalistic intelligence in a tangible way to our students.

As populations rapidly migrate from rural to urban environments, we're connecting with nature far less frequently than in the past. Libraries that incorporate plants and living things within their settings can help remind us of our connection to nature and our place within a larger ecosystem. To highlight nature and students' naturalistic intelligence in our libraries, we'll need to facilitate learning that can help students find solutions to the devastation of our natural environment.

NATURALISTIC INTELLIGENCE

Dr. Howard Gardner originally proposed seven intelligences but his research led him to propose an eighth intelligence in the 1990s: naturalistic intelligence. This type of intelligence involves a keen receptiveness to the ecological surroundings in which we find ourselves and involves the ability to carefully observe and understand the processes of plant and animal systems. Teacher and consultant Bruce Campbell at Johns Hopkins School of Education states, "This intelligence has to do with observing, understanding and organizing patterns in the natural environment. A naturalist is someone who shows expertise in the recognition and classification of plants and animals."

We hope to create an avatar for our naturalistic area modeled after someone like Jane Goodall, PhD, who helped set up our school's Roots & Shoots program (rootsandshoots.org).

The avatar we plan to create might introduce the area in this manner:

> The space you are entering is called the 'Living Room,' and it is a metaphor for nature and our desire to awaken your naturalistic intelligence. This era of civilization has largely ignored nature. And in recent years, human beings have sought to dominate nature, rather than understand their role within it. The truth is, though, we cannot harm nature without harming ourselves. We have largely ignored the devastating effects of global pollution, global warming, overpopulation, and species extinction. We ask that you take time to awaken your naturalistic intelligence and begin actively observing and interacting with the natural environment around you—you will become more human in doing so.

If you want to learn more about naturalistic intelligence, talk to your school's science teachers, visit their classrooms, and discuss their curriculum. Host a lunch and see if you can talk them into helping set up a naturalistic corner in your library, where you can feature books about some of the biggest issues facing the planet today, including climate change; air, land, and water pollution; species extinction; and resource depletion. This area could even serve as the headquarters for an ecology club or spark a recycling effort in the school.

Additionally, "Naturalistic Intelligence Strategies," a list developed by Bruce Campbell at Johns Hopkins School of Education offers a wealth of ideas for incorporating elements from nature into your learning spaces: bit.ly/2mkqYXa.

TOOLKIT FOR EXPLORING NATURE

- Ant farms: Myrmecology, or the study of ants' behavior, can lead to insights about social networks.

- Aquariums: These are popular and instructive in classrooms and libraries.

- Charts: Periodic tables, animal kingdom charts, etc., are helpful to illustrate nature.

- Greenhouse boxes: These can be built in a maker area to introduce students to plant life.

- Insect specimens: They may be labeled and mounted in cases for display.

- Microscopes: These are handy tools in a naturalistic area.

- Molecular models: These 3-D images illustrate nature on a micro-scale.

- Telescopes: These are great tools for libraries to loan in areas where star-gazing is good.

CHAPTER 20

Know Thyself and Others

*Everything that irritates us about others can lead us to an
understanding of ourselves.*

—C.G. Jung

L et's get personal. In *Frames of Mind*, Howard Gardner
places interpersonal intelligence and intrapersonal intelligence
together in one chapter titled "The Personal Intelligences." So
why create two intelligences if they could be grouped together as one?
Because, as he shows through his work, although they develop side-
by-side in a symbiotic relationship, they operate in separate, distinct
ways. And to illustrate these forms' distinctions, he provides evidence
of neurological brain structures, cultural and symbol systems, psycho-
metric evidence, and human-development studies.

Know Thyself

The ancient Greek maxim, "Know thyself" represents the very essence of intrapersonal intelligence. If you have a good understanding of your own feelings, motives, identity, and sense of self, you have a firm foundation to guide your actions. However, this alone is not enough, as we are social creatures and we must harmonize and work with others to adapt and survive. That's why interpersonal intelligence works hand-in-hand with intrapersonal intelligence, allowing us to grasp, empathize, and adapt to other people's thinking and behavioral patterns, which is equally as crucial to our survival.

Zen Librarian

As we adopt the more collaborative workspaces discussed in this book, we risk losing our libraries' Zen nature. Historically, libraries have been excellent places for quiet introspection and reflection. And although noise is becoming a more acceptable feature, especially as we encourage interaction, we still need to offer patrons tranquil spaces for self-reflection and quiet study. After all, we need places where we can relax and focus without interruption.

Inner Space

Intrapersonal intelligence refers to our introspective and self-reflective capacities. Developing this intelligence requires us to have a deep understanding of ourselves, what our strengths and weaknesses are, and what makes us unique. By developing our intrapersonal intelligence, we can cue into our own reactions and emotions.

Plato's Caves

We could argue that libraries play a role in supporting intrapersonal intelligence simply by providing quiet spaces and literature on philosophy, religion, psychology, and other disciplines exploring human nature, but we can do better.

When my colleagues and I sought to create a specific zone for intrapersonal intelligence in our library, we ran into a problem: our new collaborative spirit had caught on so well that our students wanted to talk and visit in this new space. We needed to present a new viewpoint much different from our more extroverted zones. So, we decided to set up several individualized spaces with chairs like the ones below.

Bubble chair   **Egg chair**

Imagine providing opportunities within your library for members to not only have places for introspection and self-reflection but also to access tools for self-assessment and gain a deeper personal understanding of themselves. Your area might even include biofeedback or neurofeedback equipment to help members with stress reduction. You could partner with your school's counseling or psychology department to create this area. School counselors are great resources for tools, resources, and experience in helping others to communicate and listen more effectively.

The Soft Parade

Marketing your intrapersonal spaces can be a bit tricky; if too many people find out about them, they will cease to be places of tranquility and simply become new areas for noisy collaboration. So, to protect these spaces, we must establish norms to help patrons understand that these are quiet zones of reflection. Best-selling author Susan Cain says in her book, *Quiet*, that approximately a third of the United States' population is estimated to be introverted, with the remaining two-thirds being more extroverted. Introverts are among the most loyal supporters of libraries, so we cannot abandon them; rather, we must actively protect their needs within this changing landscape.

What Is Your EQ?

In 1996, I heard Daniel Goleman, PhD, speak on emotional intelligence at Harvard University. Goleman talked about EQ as being able to read people and understand their emotions and points of view. He said that individuals with a high emotional quotient could communicate well with others, had good self-understanding, and were good listeners. In reading that I have done since that time, EQ sounds very much like a combination of Gardner's interpersonal intelligence and intrapersonal intelligence. Goleman, who is a best-selling author, spoke well and was charismatic and persuasive—he seemed to be the very embodiment of emotional intelligence. Goleman's work shows that our "emotional quotient" (EQ) may be even more important to our job performance and overall success in life than our "intelligence quotient" (IQ). He says the keys to this success are being able to relate to others, read social cues, and understand people.

TOOLKIT FOR INTROVERTS
See page 276 for links.

- **Personality tests:** TheMuse.com offers a variety of personality tests to help readers better understand themselves.

- **Virtual counseling:** Researchers are exploring how virtual therapists may help people talk freely during counseling sessions.

- **The Human Library:** At humanlibrary.org, talk to people and learn about others' points of view.

- **Biofeedback or neurofeedback**: Allow users to learn stress-reduction techniques.

- **Biometrics**: Provide users with feedback on health and exercise.

- **Digital portfolios**: These promote self-monitoring and self-directed learning.

- **Journal writing**: This is an excellent way to promote personal growth and reflection.

- **Mindfulness training**: Make this available through podcasts, software, and books.

HOW DO YOU FEEL ABOUT THAT?

People whose strengths lie in their interpersonal intelligence often enjoy a good discussion or debate and typically learn best by working with others. Gardner says that's because this type of intelligence reflects our ability to recognize and understand people's moods, desires, feelings, temperaments, motivations, and intentions. And, in theory, those individuals possessing a high level of interpersonal intelligence are characterized by how well they cooperate and work as part of a group.

By transforming libraries into a sort of "community commons," where people meet, learn, communicate, and collaborate, we can facilitate communication, critical thinking, collaboration, innovation, and awareness of human issues and help our members increase their interpersonal intelligence.

THE PIER POINT

Traditional libraries discourage talking, as they believe it interferes with silent reading and study. Libraries of the future, though, will need to provide flexible arrangements to accommodate patrons' increasingly varied needs, from reading and studying to collaborating and interacting.

Remember this: providing support and facilitating learning in all eight forms of intelligence is no easy task, so don't sweat the small stuff—just do what you can to help your patrons. What works in one library may be a disaster in another. Fortunately, since interpersonal intelligence involves a certain sensitivity to others' needs and feelings, the task of balancing patrons' interpersonal situations helps you develop your own interpersonal intelligence. For example, how can your library create a positive vibe and a welcoming feeling for both first-time and frequent visitors?

We can also encourage collaborative work by supporting members' project initiatives, including organizations, activities, and projects, promoting social awareness and personal communication.

People need places to gather and socialize. Although social media fills a need for interpersonal communication, there is still a burning need for direct, face-to-face human contact. This is where libraries can help.

By creating a commons area within our libraries, we can encourage the informal communication necessary for friendships to form and ideas to evolve. When we have the opportunity to meet people in relaxed, safe surroundings, we can further develop our interpersonal skills and EQ. Team up with your school's counselors, sports coaches, and club advisors, and together, promote social interaction in a relaxed, comfortable, and safe setting, the kind of place all sorts of people can feel at home in when they enter.

The name I came up with for an interpersonal zone was the "Meeting Point." I'd envisioned it as a place students could hold meetings and feel welcome to just stop by. (I suppose if this had been in a high school, this space might evolve into the "Dating Point," and that wouldn't be such a bad thing.) One of the school's counselors asked if the peer counselors could have a place in the library for their meetings so they could become a visible presence among the students. The students changed the name from the "Meeting Point" to the "Pier Point," and in doing so, took charge of deciding how that space would evolve. We are stilling working to create the right setting for Pier Point. To be honest, the space we selected was on the quiet side of the library, and the lively group interaction was at odds with our desire to have quiet study space. We decided that so much interaction and socializing happens in a good way on our collaborative side of the library that we would create an area enclosed by bookcases as the new Pier Point.

OPENING FOR AN AVATAR, HIRING NOW

We still need to design an avatar for our interpersonal intelligence area. The nice thing about avatars is that you can shape their personalities and mold them into whichever character you desire. Designing a suitable avatar for interpersonal intelligence might lead you to look at occupations and characters who communicate well and have good interpersonal skills. TV talk show hosts certainly fit the bill, as do counselors, therapists, and others in the social sciences. We all have friends who are spark plugs for conversations and motivate others around them to share and interact, so you could model your avatar after one of them. Perhaps a character like famed motivational speaker Tony Robbins could get the conversation rolling or maybe a teenage figure, who listens well and is approachable and relatable, would work better.

As you design your avatar, also think of the audience it be speaking to. In my case, my library serves eleven- to thirteen-year-olds, so I design avatars that preteens can relate to. Now, ideally, the avatar would be interactive and could respond to questions and not simply be a talking head. While this is possible given the current state of technology, fully interactive avatars are difficult to design and implement. So, as a starting point, I suggest sticking with avatars that can only talk to students, not respond to comments.

THE HUMAN LIBRARY

"The Human Library is designed to build a positive framework for conversations that can challenge stereotypes and prejudices through dialogue," proclaims humanlibrary.org. The site asks people to volunteer as "books" and serve as resources for "readers" interested in a book's perspective on their religion, politics, human-rights situations, or any number of other issues.

For example, you might have a quadriplegic willing to answer questions from someone who wants to better understand what life is like without use of their arms and legs. Or the "book" could be a Muslim, Christian, someone who has been adopted, or someone who has been a refugee. Whatever the case, these "books" speak about their beliefs from their perspectives based on their firsthand experiences.

The Human Library is an edgy, exciting concept, to be sure, but don't think it is something I would try with my middle school students. That said, I do think it could initiate productive conversations with library members who have had enough life experience to grasp the abstract and the very real elements of the issues discussed. We might use teachers as the human books at the middle school level, or we might have high school students trying out this idea in a high school library setting.

THREE-RING OR EIGHT-RING CIRCUS

Libraries have the challenging task of trying to provide good settings for a variety of people who sometimes have conflicting needs. Case in point: some members come to our libraries to meet friends or do hands-on projects in small groups, while others come in to find a good book and seek a quiet place in which to read.

In our library, my colleagues and I run what feels like an eight-ring circus as we try to facilitate all eight forms of intelligence while trying to ensure everyone gets along. This is not always possible, and we do have to make compromises from time to time. As you begin designing your library, your members will have different demands, and you, too, will have to make compromises to best serve as many members as possible. Whether you run a three- or an eight-ring circus, you will most certainly have to deal with two categories of people: those who want quiet, reflective spaces and those who want dynamic, collaborative zones. With proper care and attention, it is possible to develop library settings into places that accommodate introverts and extroverts alike.

CHAPTER 21

Virtually There

We do not stop playing because we grow old; we grow old because we stop playing!

—Benjamin Franklin

Storytelling is so fundamental to our nature as human beings that it seems almost innate. We tell stories to relate our experiences to one another. We tell stories to express how we're feeling and how we're reacting to events in the world. We tell stories to better understand who we are and to uncover our personal narrative that lies at the core of our existence.

Most online games are a form of storytelling, and as Shakespeare said, "All the world's a stage, and all the men and women merely players. " Online games have all the elements of storytelling within them: characters involved in adventures and conflict, issues involving good and evil, as well as (usually) a quest and a struggle to overcome odds. While some games develop their storylines better than others, I think it's fair to say they all resemble stories in one fashion or another. For this reason, the ALA urges librarians to embrace online gaming and recognize it as a valid form of learning.

New Media Consortium's Horizon Project's 2011 *Horizon Report* says game-based learning "has gained considerable traction since 2003, when James Gee began to describe the impact of game play on cognitive development...Proponents of game-based learning in higher education point to its role in supporting collaboration, problem solving, and communication." The work of James Gee, PhD, who is a professor of reading at the University of Wisconsin, was cited by the *Horizon Report* as supporting gaming as a valuable form of storytelling and problem solving.

Will game-based learning work at your school? Do we want it in our classrooms? Let's first try it in our libraries so that we can observe its pros and cons before making any final decisions. As librarians, we need to take great care to provide the same protections from censorship of gaming as we apply to other informational sources. By using libraries as testing grounds, schools can be much more experimental and not have to risk disrupting or harming the curriculum.

The "serious games movement" offers schools opportunities to address social issues, such as exploration for oil, environmental simulations, music-melody compositions, climate change, and population issues. *The 2011 Horizon Report* goes on to say that:

> Open-ended, challenge-based, truly collaborative games
> have tremendous potential to transform higher education...
> Games like these, which occur in both massively multiplayer
> online (MMO) and non-digital forms, can draw on skills for
> research, writing, collaboration, problem solving, public speak-
> ing, leadership, digital literacy, and media making. When
> embedded in the curriculum, they offer a path into the material

that allows the student to learn how to learn along with mastering and truly owning the subject matter.

Author, futurist, and game designer Jane McGonigal, PhD, argues that harnessing video games' power and problem-solving strategy could have a major effect on life in the real world. "Gamers always believe that an epic win is possible," she said in her 2010 TED Talk. "Gaming can make a better world."

She describes four things virtuoso gamers gain:

- **Urgent optimism**: Gamers have an urgent motivation to act now. They believe an epic win is always worth trying now.

- **Social fabric**: Gamers usually form bonds with fellow gamers. Playing games with others helps builds trust, cooperation, and stronger social relationships.

TOOLKIT FOR GAME-BASED LEARNING
See page 279 for links.

- **Institute of Play**: Provides professional development for educators
- **MIT's Education Arcade**: An innovation center for games and simulations for learning
- **OpenAI**: A nonprofit organization for AI research
- Peacemaker: An online game for problem solving the issues of peace
- **Quest to Learn**: Provides middle and high school students with game-based problem solving
- **TensorFlow**: An open-source artificial intelligence software for developing games

- **Blissful productivity**: Gamers are actually happier working hard than when they are relaxing and doing nothing.

- **Epic meaning**: Gamers love to take on grand challenges. They are super-empowered, hopeful individuals.

McGonigal believes these features of adaptability are achieved through gaming and are transferable to real life.

LEARNING SPACE

Thanks to virtual reality (VR) and augmented reality (AR) devices, such as the Oculus Rift, HoloLens, HTC Vive, Meta 2, we can now enter digital worlds and experience new environments that are so vivid, our brains believe what we're seeing is real. Though VR can include gaming, it can also just as easily model real-world environments, allowing us to try new skills, new places, and new experiences without the normal dangers and risks associated with them.

VR has moved from clunky, slow, distorted images to highly realistic, compelling environments that allow us to sky dive, fight in wars, travel into space, and talk to famous authors, scientists, and world leaders in safe, comfortable environments. No doubt about it, this medium will become a major learning tool in the next few years. My own experiences with the Oculus Rift have convinced me of this.

As Meta founder and CEO Meron Gribetz explains in his 2016 TED Talk, AR offers us "a glimpse of the future through an augmented reality headset," and transforms and enhances our experience of everyday reality. Furthermore, AR allows us to become the operating system, to touch and see in ways that trigger our sense of proprioception or neural connections and collaborate in new ways through what he calls a holographic campfire echoing Thornburg's campfires in cyberspace.

HoloLens is a unique device produced by Microsoft that combines VR with AR to offer great possibilities for learning. Recently, our library and technology staffs had an opportunity to try the HoloLens.

It is a lightweight pair of glasses that allows you to walk around and to view a fantasy VR environment, while also incorporating people and objects from the real world. Wearing the HoloLens is a rather remarkable experience. You are transported into a strange interface between the real world, VR, and AR. It is all a bit confusing but most enjoyable to play and interact with.

Will VR or AR become addictive? Yes, of course, but addictions are common with almost all elements of life, including food, sex, exercise, TV, and the Internet. We need to learn how to control our impulses and safeguard against addictions but not abandon powerful learning tools because of the dangers that come with them. Just as all tools may be used for good or for evil, all new technologies offer risks and rewards.

I, ROBOT

In his classic novel, *I, Robot*, science-fiction writer Isaac Asimov foresaw potential ethical issues as humans began interacting with robots possessing artificial intelligence (AI). Asimov put forth the following three laws for robots to explain how humans will need to place restrictions on robots to prevent human-machine conflicts, and especially to avoid the common scenario of robots or machines conquering and possibly destroying humanity. Here are the rules:

1. A robot may not injure a human being or, through inaction, allow a human being to come to harm.
2. A robot must obey the orders given to it by human beings, except where such orders would conflict with the First Law.
3. A robot must protect its own existence as long as such protection does not conflict with the First or Second Law.

AI sounds like fake intelligence, but it's actually a different type of intelligence. We may discover more about what it means to be human by interacting with machine intelligence. Am I siding with machines when I should be standing up for humanity? I honestly don't know. Let's look further at AI, or "machine intelligence."

MR. ROBOTO

We have a couple of toy robots in the library made by WowWee called "Robosapiens." They are, of course, real robots, but they are also sold in toy stores and are limited to sixty-four commands. We plan to add a robot known as Jibo, a small and relatively inexpensive social robot who acts like a personal assistant and has the ability to interact with you in a very human way. We expect Jibo will be a good greeter at our circulation desk and may encourage conversations about books to occur. Robots ranging in price from $100 to hundreds of thousands of dollars are now available on the market and are beginning to embody sophisticated AI, allowing them to problem solve and to perform an increasingly complex range of functions.

Imagine interacting with a robot that empathizes with you, that can think (or at least process information) a thousand times faster than you, and is your loyal assistant with endless patience and tools. Yeah, I know I'm leaving out the Terminator scenario, where the same robot decides you are so stupid that he is going to just eliminate you from the equation. Let's hope Asimov's laws work.

Wired magazine co-founder Kevin Kelly presents many interesting perspectives on this in his book, *The Inevitable*, which advances on a theme of technological evolution that he put forth in his previous book called *What Technology Wants*. In *The Inevitable*, Kelly looks at our growing relationship with machines and the ways in which humans and machines can function together in a collaborative relationship. He helps to dispel the common dystopian vision that so many books and movies portray of evil machines ruling humankind. He does not ignore the dangers of AI, but views it like other powerful technologies, which can be used for good as well as evil. According to Kelly, "An AI will think about food differently than any chef, allowing us to think about food differently. Or to think about manufacturing materials differently.... As AIs develop, we might have to engineer ways to *prevent* consciousness in them—our most premium AI services will be advertised as *consciousness-free.*"

Several libraries have introduced robots into their community-technology offerings, including Connecticut's Westport Library. "Robotics is the next disruptive technology coming into our lives and we felt it was important to make it accessible to people so they could learn about it," the library's now-former executive director, Maxine Bleiweis, told the *Wall Street Journal* in 2014.

Robots are here to stay, so we better start designing them to be protectors and helpers of humanity, rather than villains or opponents. Libraries can offer more services, more expertise, and more staff through the introduction of robotic technology. They can also allow students and other patrons time to explore and understand this technology, allowing us engage in informed conversations about the role we want robots to play in society and work.

VIRTUAL AND AUGMENTED

In their article for the Harvard Business Review's website titled, "Virtual and Augmented Reality Will Reshape Retail," L.E.K. Consulting's Dan McKone, Robert Haslehurst, and Maria Steingoltz offer an example of two individuals shopping online and both crawling into a tent together. The surprising part was that one person was in Boston and the other was in Houston. Through computer-generated images (CGI), VR creates immersive computer-generated environments and offers opportunities for learning to occur in settings and circumstances that would be otherwise impossible to arrange.

My library currently has two early versions of the Oculus Rift, a VR headset. Students sign up to reserve the headgear and can then access a wide number of programs that simulate everything from flying a helicopter to space travel. I recently went on a voyage through the artery of a human heart and could look in any direction and see what it's like traveling through the tube-shaped artery.

Augmented reality, on the other hand, augments the real-world imagery it receives through a video lens by adding text, graphics, sounds, haptic feedback, and sometimes even smell. A good example of a simple AR application is the Pokémon GO app, which adds Pokémon characters to the actual environment that the user captures, using their phone or other mobile device.

In 2016, I attended the New Age Learning Spaces conference in Singapore, where New Media Consortium CEO Larry Johnson gave a great talk on emerging technologies. Toward the end of his presentation, he mentioned the Pokémon GO craze. My colleague, James McMullen, pulled out his phone, accessed the game, and found a Pokémon hovering right next to the speaker's podium. Much to the audience's amazement, he held up his screen, showing the Pokémon

TOOLKIT FOR
VIRTUAL AND AUGMENTED REALITIES
See page 279 for links.

- **Google Arts & Culture:** An amazing VR art collection
- **Google Cardboard:** Inexpensive VR viewers to use with your smartphone
- **HoloLens:** Microsoft's device that combines VR and AR
- **HTC Vive VR headset:** One of many new VR products on the market
- **Oculus Rift:** We currently demo VR in our library using this device
- **Meta 2:** An AR development kit

character near Johnson. Most of the adults in the room had never even seen the Pokémon character, though I'm sure their children at home were probably quite familiar with it.

"Augmented books are also gaining traction," says the 2011 Horizon Report. "Developers at the Gwangju Institute of Science and Technology have created a format that allows 3-D characters to emerge from the pages of books." MIT's media labs have an amazing array of projects investing the applications of gaming, robotics, and other emerging technologies to further learning in our schools. The MIT Schiller Teacher Education Program provides educators with solid research on the implications of new technologies on learning and how to implement and evaluate their use in our libraries and educational settings.

REALITY RON MEETS CYBER RON

We're going through a transition, where our perceptions of reality and our perceptions of ourselves are beginning to change. We've moved from living in a world influenced by radio to TV to the Internet, each time, creating changes along the way, but now we're learning how to function as both physical analog entities and social media personalities. Though the changes have been fairly gentle so far, as we continue entering into VR and AR spaces, they will be much more profound. And as we find ourselves completing simple transactions at the grocery store, telephone company, etc., with the help of avatars, we will be preparing for dealing with robots who exhibit better manners and social skills than our own.

In *The Singularity Is Near*, Kurzweil predicts a not-too-distant future where we will interact with avatars, robots, and even androids (humans with augmented robotic features). He predicts human and machine intelligence, or AI, will blur the lines between carbon-based creatures, such as ourselves, and our silicon creations. And while most

AI researchers foresee artificial intelligence surpassing human intelligence in the not-too-distant future, not all are as optimistic as Kurzweil about humanity's fate.

Mathematician Stephen Hawking, Microsoft co-founder Bill Gates; and entrepreneur Elon Musk have all expressed concerns about the possibility of humanity being dominated by higher-functioning machine intelligence. But in an article published by *The Telegraph* titled "Elon Musk: Become Cyborgs or Risk Humans Being Turned into Robots' Pets," Musk did not advise that we run away from AI, but instead he focused on ways we could augment human capabilities. Musk said that as artificial intelligence advances, "People will need to augment their brain power with digital technology to prevent them [from] becoming irrelevant."

As librarians, we can choose to hide our heads in the sand or play a part in deciding how to shape this technology in ways benefiting humanity.

A few years ago, I saw a comedian perform some zany material that I loved. One scene that absolutely fascinated me, though, involved him talking to his partner pictured on a television set facing him. I vowed right then and there, "I am going to do that!" Thus, "Reality Ron" and "Cyber Ron" were created.

My hope was that by bringing Reality Ron and Cyber Ron to life, I could captivate students' imaginations and encourage them to think about books and the Internet and how the two worlds are not so far apart. With the help of a colleague named Dave Hevey, a film production teacher, I videotaped myself carrying on both sides of a dialog. Dave and I first filmed the Cyber Ron character, who was dressed in beach gear (shorts, T-shirt, hat, and sunglasses), talking about his life in cyberspace. With the help of a green screen, we had stars flying in the background behind him. Then we filmed Reality Ron, who was dressed in a shirt and tie.

Here's how it played out:

Reality Ron: (Stands in front of a large projection screen facing Cyber Ron, who is thoughtfully listening.) "Welcome to the reality of middle school, and welcome to my doppelgänger, Cyber Ron from cyberspace. Today, we are going to explore the world of the book."

Cyber Ron: "Uh, hi. Reality Ron, what the heck is a book and how does it work? Does it run on Wi-Fi or Bluetooth?"

Reality Ron: "Nope, it's analog—you just read the pages and the information scans directly into your brain."

Cyber Ron: "Wow! May I see that?"

Reality Ron: (Appears to hand the book to Cyber Ron, but actually places it on a bench behind the screen.)

This conversation touched on aspects of the print and digital worlds, and in the end, Cyber Ron asked Reality Ron if he could take over for him in cyberspace for a while, as he was going on a date with an avatar named Zelda in Second Life. Reality Ron gamely agreed, so he jumped behind the screen and into cyberspace, bounding into the video wearing the same outfit he was wearing in reality.

This video was a hit, and it helped my middle school students visualize the two worlds they live in, as well as how different "reality" can look from each perspective. As we move between VR, AR, and other digital worlds back into the physical world, things will look just a bit different, similar to what Reality Ron and Cyber Ron experienced. Students liked the video because it incorporated humor with instruction and it showed how reading books is still relevant even in the age of Internet. When Reality Ron says, "Look, I can scan and download the ideas of this page directly into my brain through reading," they get the joke and they see how this process is equally or more amazing than computer downloads on hardware.

GESTURE-BASED COMPUTING

When you use an iPad or other touch screen device, the software allows you to perform different functions based on the way you touch the screen, say with a swipe to the left or right or up or down. In gesture-based computing, a camera eye, lens, or a sensor attached to your hand can interpret movements that you make in the air as computer commands. This allows for a much more fluid and creative way of interacting with technology. As early as 2009, Patti Maes, an instructor at MIT, demonstrated a device called the SixthSense in a TED talk titled "Pattie Maes + Pranav Mistry: Meet the SixthSense Interaction." The device was developed by her student Pranav Mistry. To date, this remains one of the best demonstrations of the capability of gesture-based computers that I know of. Pranav Mistry has moved on to other projects, but no doubt his "SixthSense" will augment the ways in which we use gesture-based computing in everyday life. In libraries,

TOOLKIT FOR
ARTIFICIAL INTELLIGENCE
See page 280 for links.

- **"2016 Will Be a Pivotal Year for Social Robots":** Jibo, Pepper, and friends are on the way

- **"Brain-Computer Interface That Works Wirelessly":** Demonstrates a wireless brain-to-computer interface

- **Human-Computer Interaction Resources:** Has more than 126,000 articles on the topic

- **Reactable:** A multi-touch interface for playing music

- **WowWee Rovio Robotic WebCam:** Roaming drone provides audio and video for example, we can place QR codes on books with embedded video, text, or photos to aid in browsing and marketing books.

CHAPTER 22

Phoenix Rising

Culture eats strategy for breakfast.

—Peter Drucker

Books all too often imply that institutional change is simple and painless. "Sure, just follow these easy steps and you can transform your library into an innovation center before the end of the school year." *Ah, if it were only that simple.*

Libraries represent different things to different people, and as a librarian, it's your job to try and meet a diverse population's needs while balancing off fairly well-entrenched ideas about your role and what a library should and should not be. Schools are politically charged environments, and you can bet the ideas in this book will challenge some people's current thinking. Many of the ideas I'm presenting have taken years to refine and achieve, and to be honest, some still aren't working as well as I'd like. My staff and I have had so many failures that there isn't enough time to discuss them all. Our biggest failure, though, was also our greatest success. It was called "The Connections Project."

The Connections Project

In 2008, I submitted a proposal to build a mezzanine in our library so we could create four learning design studios, which would serve as high-tech workspaces for small groups of students. I made a few modifications and submitted the proposal again in 2009. In 2010, Mike Pelletier, our school's computer coordinator, shared some ideas he'd been developing for creating an R&D center for emerging technologies. We combined the two concepts and started drawing up plans for what we called "Connections" or "The Connections Project."

We then formed a professional learning community with several faculty members and met on a weekly basis for well over a year. In 2011, a larger implementation committee, which included administrators and teachers, formed, and the project quickly gained traction and grew much faster than we expected. The plan increased dramatically in scope and in financial cost.

Dream Workshops

Once we received approval to develop a new design for the library, we met with a well-respected architectural firm and started the planning process. This highly innovative team conducted "dream workshops" with our teachers, administrators, students, and parents in conversations about their ideal learning spaces and how those ideas relate to libraries.

Here's a sampling of opinions gained from the dream workshops:

- **Books are still precious and relevant.** There is an element of serendipity when you look for information in a large collection of books.

- **"Library" and "librarian" are no longer adequate terms** to encapsulate and communicate the scope and depth of learning opportunities desired in this setting.

- **Students and teachers thrive in relationship-building**, which can be supported through engaged learning environments that bring real, authentic experiences into a safe, curated platform.

- **Everyone shares similar definitions of "learning,"** all of which are based on growth, exploration, and experimentation. Learning often involves taking a risk and doing something you haven't done before.

- **Connection and community are no longer defined by physical space and proximity**. An ideal learning space would be an environment that helps learners to further connect to the world.

- **Fun and games are essential to every student's learning experience**. We should strive to create innovative spaces that allow for play and experimentation.

- **A unique school experience is defined by what is offered outside of its core curriculum**. The library can help individualize and personalize learning opportunities.

- **Libraries should visually strike a balance of being inspirational, intimate, and comforting**. Participants stressed the need for a comfortable, inviting, and friendly setting.

- **Learning is not defined through controlled and examined output**, but through process, reflection, and independent expressions of knowledge. There's a sense of ownership and empowerment for kids when left to choose and create their own curriculum.

As a result of these comments and reflections, we gained the confidence we needed to make some significant changes in our library. Involving our stakeholders in the process helped generate ideas and made everyone more actively involved and informed.

Our Vision Statement

Our library, referred to here as "The Connection," will redefine our approach to learning and the pedagogy we value and use at Singapore American School. This proposal seeks to redesign the middle school library and our organizational structure. The Connection Team will work with students and teachers in the development of twenty-first-century skills. The Connection will promote and encourage creativity and innovation, communication and collaboration, research and information fluency, critical thinking and problem solving, digital citizenship, and lifelong learning.

Our vision is to connect people and ideas, to connect the arts and the sciences, to connect literature with social concerns, and to connect our curriculum with new social media and emerging technologies. In short, we intend to redesign learning and teaching to better meet the demands of the twenty-first century. We believe the library can serve as the "connection" and stimulus for developing these forward-thinking practices in the school.

Fostering a Community of Learners

The Connection is designed to foster a community of learners; it serves as a global classroom, a global hub, and a collaboration center. Every individual is viewed as a learner, regardless of societal roles. The Connection is a unique hybrid combining elements of the traditional library with those of a "creation and communications center" and a "research and development center." Teachers and students learn from each other in this setting. It is a teacher training center, an experimental classroom, and a community commons all in one.

The Connection Team will provide a critical organizational component to ensure that the introduction of emerging technologies positively and substantively impacts student learning. Library and technology staff will be oriented in twenty-first-century pedagogy and will serve as facilitators and coaches with students and teachers in discovering and developing solutions to real-world problems. The Connection Team will also serve as a research and development team in testing possibilities offered through mobile computing, augmented reality, gesture-based computing, video feedback, game-based learning, and other emerging technologies. In essence, the focus of the Connection Team will be to help students and teachers to effectively use technology to connect with knowledge, perspectives, possibilities, and opportunities throughout the world.

The Connection with Literature

Capturing and enhancing the elements of a traditional library, the "Connection with Literature" is attractive and comfortable. It offers an inviting environmental setting with an abundance of natural lighting and acoustical treatments to dampen unwanted noise. This learning zone includes a variety of innovative furniture designs appealing to young adults and teachers alike. Unique cube book shelving that interlocks and creates walls and study areas accommodates a print collection of 25,000 volumes while the SAS online digital databases offer a much larger array of informational resources. The overall design provides for ultimate flexibility, allowing for quiet individual reading, small-group work, and large-group presentations. This area includes a staff work area and pantry for accommodating a wide range of school functions.

The Connection will develop a more interactive and participatory learning environment in which the paradigm shifts from mere access to available resources to an innovative model where students and staff are encouraged to pursue authentic learning in real-life contexts through creation and innovation, communication and collaboration, and research from diverse perspectives using processes that contribute to critical thinking and problem solving. Students and staff will have the opportunity to connect with the world in a unique learning environment. The end result will be adaptable twenty-first-century learners who are global citizens with a passion for lifelong learning.

STUDENTS WILL:

- Have more opportunities for challenge-based learning.
- Be allowed to make mistakes and to play with new ideas and approaches to learning.
- Have more opportunities to experiment with new emerging technologies.
- Have more hands-on, right-brain performance-based learning.
- Be involved in more cross-disciplinary work.

TEACHERS WILL:

- Gain the support of a team approach to instructional development.
- Have faster and more convenient access to new emerging technologies.
- Have more opportunities for just-in-time professional development.
- Be able to access state-of-the-art facilities to support them in new curricular designs.
- Gain feedback on their teaching through videotaped sessions.
- Be better able to differentiate instruction.

THE SCHOOL WILL:

- Save money by testing out new technology before adopting hardware or software across all divisions.

- Develop a knowledge-management system that allows the staff to do a better job of sharing the best ideas and best practices in the school.

- Accommodate a larger number of students with fewer classrooms by better utilizing the library facilities.

- Try out new curricular models in a safe, well-documented environment before adopting such practices school wide.

THE DISCONNECTION

In May 2012, at the height of the project, our planning team flew to San Francisco to meet with experts at Apple, Google, and CISCO headquarters.

Decisions had already been made back in Singapore, and our project was placed on hold. The school board was split in their support for the project, and we were also in the process of transitioning from one superintendent to a new one. Although both superintendents were in favor of the plan, since it had grown so large in scope, it required outside funding. The school did not follow up on a large grant offer from Cisco as too many other projects were already happening across the school, so we found ourselves in limbo for about two years. In that time, we lost several key members of our group, and enthusiasm for the project shifted to other more pressing needs in the school. It seemed as though we were watching a thousand hours of work go down the drain. All the features of the stages of experiencing dying came into play: denial, anger, bargaining, depression, and eventually acceptance.

Learning from Failure

The first year after our postponement, our whole school launched into an R&D process that seemed to be covering much of the same ground our Connections team had already crossed. It was as though we'd been waiting for the rest of the school to catch up.

After a year of visiting other schools and hearing from a number of visiting consultants, we decided our ideas were still viable. And as you've read in this book, we redesigned the Connections model and adopted Gardner's multiple intelligences theory as a way to facilitate student learning. We work on new ideas every day, but on a smaller, lower-cost scale. And, as it turns out, the time we spent researching was not wasted—it actually proved to be highly valuable.

Here is a quick summary of what we learned:

- There is no such thing as the "perfect library" or "perfect school."

- As Nike says, "Just do it." Move beyond ideation to action as quickly as possible. Too many meetings and too much brainstorming can kill initiative.

- Vow to do no harm, and then avoid asking for permission. Instead, ask for forgiveness. If you ask permission for every bold idea you have, then you are placing your supervisor in an awkward position. After all, why should they assume responsibility for your risks?

- Track your innovation's progress, and don't tackle too much at one time. Rather, carefully ensure that you prototype, test, and evaluate before assuming the tree you've planted will grow.

- Recognize that programs rarely perform as well as they are presented in books, videos, or tours. (Yes, that applies to this book, too.)

- Be willing to make adjustments based on feedback.

- Let go of your ego as much as possible. The library does not belong to you; it is a shared civic space that must respond to the community's needs.

- Remember, you are not in competition with other programs or libraries; you will gain far more through collaboration.

- Don't be afraid to share your secrets. Obtain copyrights when prudent, but realize you are likely to gain more from putting your ideas out there than keeping them secret.

- Get beyond your own sugar-coated utopian vision and make careful, unbiased observations as you evaluate your progress and improve your services.

- Money is helpful, but it brings its own problems. If you throw too much money at a problem, the scale and risk become larger. Big money makes us more cautious.

- Go for small-scale solutions and test several iterations. Start with cardboard before attempting the solution with bricks and mortar. You can be much more fluid, agile, and able to take risks when you start with simple, low-cost experiments.

- Keep in contact with and gain empathy from your stakeholders. Find out their needs, their fears, and their desires. Test each new idea with a few people before adopting wide-scale change.

- Look for good ideas that you can adopt for your library—look in shopping malls, museums, bookstores, science centers, amusement parks, and wherever else you see innovation happening.

- Seek the best tools for learning. Read, research, watch TED Talks, follow blogs, talk to innovators, and keep abreast of new and emerging technologies.

- Avoid dogma, doctrine, and fixed ideas about pedagogy or learning. Libraries need to continue pursuing a balanced view by providing access to differing perspectives and approaches.

- Have a clear understanding of why you are doing things. In *Winning*, best-selling author Jack Welch notes that "trying to be all things to all people at all times" is an all-too-common trap.

REFLECTION

Looking back on this experience, I am happy with where we are and where we're going. I would have loved to have seen the full Connections Project implemented, but I can see how we needed more time to test our theories and work out nuts-and-bolts decisions. If a school had the proper staff and financial resources, I still think the full project could be a game-changer for implementing dynamic curriculum change.

That said, if you're contemplating large systemic changes within your school, start small and grow slowly. Money is great, but it often gets in the way, as the process becomes more bureaucratic and committee-driven, which can cause you to lose your passion for the project. If you have an idea that you strongly believe has merit and will benefit society, then you have an obligation to yourself and to others to see it through. You must, of course, weigh the costs and benefits, but listen to others, learn from your mistakes and failures, and don't give up on the things most important to you. Our team never gave up, and out of our disappointment, we gained experience, skills, and inspiration for excellent learning opportunities for our students.

CHAPTER 23

Just Do It

I want to stay as close to the edge as I can without going over. Out on the edge you see all kinds of things you can't see from the center.

—*Kurt Vonnegut,* **Player Piano**

Do not fear to be eccentric in opinion, for every opinion now accepted was once eccentric.

—*Bertrand Russell*

Are you a talker or a doer? Do you come up with great ideas, but never find the time to actually try them? Perhaps you need some structure to allow you to ideate, move forward, and create. My colleagues and I created the "Innovation Tracker" (Figure 23.2, page 214) to track our projects' statuses. Here's how it works: Each day, team members brainstorm new ideas they'd like to discuss and add to the tracker. Some days, we may not have any ideas or time to add to the ones we do have, and other days, we may come up with several. About once each month, we look over our list of ideas and decide which ones to pursue.

First, we remind ourselves of the library mission: "Our mission is to facilitate learning and knowledge creation. We will assist members in becoming thoughtful users and creators of information with an emphasis on improving society through lifelong learning."

Next, we look at our priorities. Some ideas may satisfy all of our priorities, while others only meet one or two. We don't have a hard-and-fast rule, but we use the following guidelines to vote as a group on which ideas to try.

Setting Priorities

1. **Low-hanging fruit**: These projects are low-cost, low-effort, and easy-to-implement, and use at-hand materials and space.
   Example: Set up Kiva Planks in a small area of the library and allow students to build structures. We already had Keva Planks and we had a suitable area, so we viewed this as low-hanging fruit.

2. **High impact**: The more students who benefit from these projects, the better.
   Example: Create a book swap bowl so any student can bring a book from home and trade it for one of the discarded books in the book swap bowl.

3. **Good fit with the curriculum**: This project correlates to a lesson plan or unit already in our curriculum.
   Example: Stage an Egyptian museum in the library involving the entire sixth-grade class.

4. **Emerging tech**: These projects create new possibilities for students (read *The Horizon Report*).
   Example: Purchase and set up an Oculus Rift as a VR station in the library for students to experiment with.

5. **Stakeholder-initiated ideas**: Form focus groups or dream workshops, interview students in the library, and solicit input on new and old learning spaces.

   Example: Establish a gaming room for students who want to engage in games such as Minecraft together.

6. **Ideas that inspire innovative thinking or contribute to a maker-creativity culture**: We do this by allowing students to wander into our design center. As they see James or Shahrin building something like a bamboo bicycle, they are invited to ask questions and to help and learn how.

   Example: Download paper cut-out models for students to construct. Provide the needed space, tools, and materials to support students.

7. **Things we have expertise on**: Tap staff members or students with a desired skill set.

   Example: Create video book trailers by teaming up students who enjoy reading with those who enjoy making videos.

8. **Sustainable:** These projects are easy for students to use and explore without needing a great deal of outside assistance.

   Example: Set up an exercise area to allow students to move.

In our Innovation Tracker, we write which stage each project is at, based on our "Product Life Cycle" (Figure 23.1, page 214). New projects always start out as a 1, "Idea is proposed." Once we've decided to try the idea, we move on to Level 2, meaning we do the project on a low-resolution level, or a small and inexpensive way, so we can see how stakeholders react. If our stakeholders like the idea and we see it as worth pursuing, then we move it to Level 3, "Near completion," during which we put more time and effort into polishing the project and making it sustainable and accessible. Some of our projects have been at Level 3 for years without any need of modification, while others have hit Level 4, "Has reached mature state," where we recognize the need to provide a refresh or revision using new equipment or a new approach. We've rated other ideas as 0, simply because we need to discontinue the project so we can make room for better ideas.

THE PRODUCT LIFE CYCLE

0 = No go: We have decided not to pursue this idea.

1 = Idea is proposed: We allow time for discussion and brainstorming pros and cons.

2 = Idea is tried at a low-resolution level: We allow time for stakeholders to offer feedback.

3 = Near completion: The project isn't quite functional and may still need some improvements.

4 = Has reached mature stage: The project is ready for revision or reincarnation, as needed.

Figure 23.1

Date	Idea, Project, Process	Ideator	Builder	Stage
Sept. 3	Oculus Rift station	Ron	Doug	3
Oct. 20	Set up a music studio	Ron/Ben	Ben	1
Nov. 12	Book swap bowl	Ron	Ron	3
Feb. 6	Make paper from scratch	Ron	James	0
March 17	Build a bamboo bike	James	James	2

Figure 23.2

In March 2015, my colleague Doug Tindall and I presented our ideas for the future of libraries at EARCOS, the East Asia Regional Council of Schools Teachers' Conference in Kota Kinabalu, Indonesia. Our presentation was well received, and we had several good conversations with other librarians working in both international and U.S. school libraries.

I was surprised and dismayed, though, by the private conversations I had with young, intelligent, and energetic librarians from schools around Southeast Asia. Their concerns about our proposals usually fell into at least one of these two categories: "We can't afford it," and "Our administration would never allow us to do that." They understood the philosophy, and many of them had better technology skills than I do— their reluctance just seemed to boil down to these two issues.

'WE CAN'T AFFORD IT'

Transforming libraries from access-driven storage warehouses to content-creating learning centers isn't necessarily costly. In fact, many of the librarians I've spoken with have student-to-librarian ratios of 450 to 1, and in the library I work in, the ratio is 950 students to 1 librarian.

While, yes, our library does have a good budget and we can afford to purchase expensive tools such as Wacom tablets, zSpace consoles, and high-quality recording equipment, they aren't necessary to implement the ideas I'm presenting in this book. It's actually quite the opposite—with a small budget and a few iPads and laptops, you can achieve miracles. In fact, I would go so far as to say that a limited budget can make you *more* innovative.

There is a grain of truth in the saying, "Necessity is the mother of invention." That's because some of our best ideas arise from desperation—we tend to be more willing to take risks if there is a low initial investment required. And sometimes money can actually get in the way, because money usually comes with strings attached.

To test an idea without spending much, simply try it in a low-resolution fashion (think building out of cardboard first before using more expensive materials), and then see how your stakeholders respond. No matter what, though, just put your idea into action—and then find out what people think about it. As librarians, we're generally viewed as careful, conservative, thoughtful individuals, not as radicals, so we can usually get away with much more than our teacher colleagues. So when we do try something new, people often assume it must be okay since the librarian is trying it.

'Our Administration Would Never Allow Us to Do That'

One could argue that many administrators have gotten where they are by not rocking the boat. If you ask for permission to try something new in the library and an administrator says "yes" and then something goes wrong, suddenly, the blame falls on their shoulders. It's no wonder some individuals in administration are more inclined to say "no" when faced with frequent requests for change. On the other hand, librarians may hold back from trying new ideas in the library and may ask for permission too frequently.

If you have researched your idea well and it is in alignment with the school's goals and mission, you might be well advised to "Just Do It." Run the idea by your colleagues, set forth a good rationale, and then try it out in a thoughtful and careful manner while observing the reactions of your stakeholders. For example, if you find visitors are disturbed by the presence of an exercise bike in the library, talk to them and explain the "why" behind it being there. Have a dialog and see if this is just a personal opinion, or if it is a concern your patrons share. In most cases, I think you'll be pleasantly surprised by the reactions of students, teachers, and administrators to honest attempts to improve the library.

Remember this: You are the person the administration hired to be your school's librarian, so you are the person responsible for making decisions about how to use the space and its resources, implementing your profession's best practices, and advocating on behalf of your library and its members. *You.* Most likely, school administrators aren't trained in library or information science, and what's more, they are usually tied up with budget concerns, issues demanding attention, staff conflicts, and outside demands.

Don't seek administrative approval, unless you really think it is necessary. In my experience, I've found school administrators are usually quite happy with changes that benefit students and that parents respond to positively. As Mahatma Gandhi said, "Be the change that you wish to see in the world."

QUICK-START, BAREBONES KIT

Since you're reading a chapter titled "Just Do It," you are either ready to buy a pair of Nikes or to make some changes in your library. You can, of course, do both.

The physical environments in which we learn significantly affect our thinking and our perceptions, a concept writer Steven Johnson illustrates well in his TED Talk, "Where Good Ideas Come From." In his TED talk, Johnson introduces us to the Grand Café in Oxford, England, which he says was the first coffeehouse to open in England in 1650. In his intro to the TED talk, Johnson says:

> *And so, effectively until the rise of the coffeehouse, you had an entire population that was effectively drunk all day. And you can imagine what that would be like, right, in your own life— and I know this is true of some of you—if you were drinking all day, and then you switched from a depressant to a stimulant in your life, you would have better ideas. You would be sharper and more alert. And so it's not an accident that a great flowering*

*of innovation happened as England switched to tea and coffee.
But the other thing that makes the coffeehouse important is the
architecture of the space. It was a space where people would get
together from different backgrounds, different fields of expertise,
and share.*

We considered adding a "Genius Café" to our library building on
the Apple idea of a place where individuals could go for help and collaboration. We were not able to adopt this idea, but there is no reason
why you can't have a go at it.

If you'd like for your library to better support collaboration, critical
thinking, and creativity, you need to take a few risks and step outside
the box. By no means do you have to go out and study architecture or
interior design, but you need to be willing to test new ideas and take
responsibility for how your learning space looks and feels.

Start by asking your students where they study at home. Find out
where they feel like they learn best and see if you can create similar
spaces in your library. You'll probably find some students need more
structured, more formal spaces, while others concentrate better in a
more homelike environment. If you're terrible at interior design, bring
in a colleague from your community and solicit their advice.

I encourage you to check out the many excellent books and websites discussing design-based thinking, including one of the my favorite
books *The Third Teacher*. Visit cool spaces in schools, libraries, museums, bookstores, coffee shops, shopping centers, and hotels for inspir-
ing ideas. Also, embrace recycling. My colleagues and I go Dumpster-
diving at our school in search of discarded, albeit still useful, items that
could be recycled or upcycled. For example, the tables in Figure 23.3
were looking out-of-date, so we decided to cut the legs down, and with
the help of our high school's art teacher, Barbara Harvey, we had the
art students paint them. (Tip: having a good collaborative relationship
with your art teacher can yield all kinds of unexpected benefits for

everyone involved.)

Figure 23.3

Remember, your library's visitors are your stakeholders, and they will be the people to either benefit from or be annoyed by your changes. So if you can adopt a scientist's attitude and engage your patrons in a dialog about learning and learning environments, they will feel as though they have a real voice in determining the type of environment they learn in, which can result in them engaging more in their own education. As you make these changes, document your work through photos and videos, thereby allowing you to show your progress, track what worked and what didn't, and share your ideas as you go along.

Now, let's imagine you work in a pretty standard, yet small, under-funded, and understaffed library. The space you have available to work with plays a fairly big role in what you can do, so there are a number of variations you can do with the ideas in this book.

Research

- Read a few of the articles mentioned in this book that most appeal to you.

Get Inspired

- Watch some of the YouTube links and TED Talks listed in this book.
- Conduct Dream Workshops,
- Involve as many people as possible.
- Offer lunch (if possible).
- Develop a dream statement based on user feedback.
- Review what you've learned.
- Select the best ideas to try.
- Identify one area to focus on, such as art, music, model building, exercise, etc.

Initiate Change

- Create a prototype: try a low-cost, easy, low-resolution solution.
- Get stakeholder feedback: see how people react to your prototype.
- Create a design: move forward with a redefined plan.
- Find "thought partners": identify teachers, students, or parents whom you could work with on your project.

Create Space

- You'll need to clear some space to allow for maker spaces, creation corners, or learning design studios.

Let's start with your collection. If you haven't done one recently, it's time to do a collection analysis, or "weeding." Most library vendors have created provisions within their automated software to help you with this task. Analyze your collection by Dewey or LC hundreds, your circulation stats, and its age. Weeding collections can be hard for many librarians—how could you possibly discard an old friend like that lovely atlas you've relied on for so long? Allow me to help: if you turn to Russia and see the "Union of Soviet Socialist Republics," it is time for that relic to retire. And sometimes you can place beautiful old books in an archives section, but be selective.

Think of weeding the way the term is intended; you are cultivating a garden, and the flowers in any garden cannot survive or be seen if they are surrounded by weeds. By removing damaged and out-of-date books, you're ensuring your library's treasures stand out.

In the high school library I worked in several years ago, we had to weed a significant number of books, but my colleagues were anxious about possible pushback we'd receive from some of our teaching staff. So I decided to organize the "Big Weed" (not a pot party). We arranged to serve everyone a nice potluck lunch and sent the invitation on the following page. We pulled all the books we thought should be weeded out and placed them on carts organized by subject area. On the day of the "Big Weed," teachers, grouped by their subject area, looked through the books and let us know which books needed to be discarded, replaced, or kept.

To help guide faculty members through the process, we also sent the following information as a Google Doc to answer our project's "why" questions:

Why are you discarding so many books?

Our main goal in weeding is to increase readership and reading. Just as in a garden, properly weeding a library makes it easier for patrons to find quality materials. Getting rid of books must sound like a strange way to increase reading, but students make snap decisions about sources. If they are looking for a good book on global current events, for example, and have to sift through outdated books that have no information about the events of the past decade, they will be turned off.

RECONSIDERATION PROCEDURE

What: "The Big Feed," or "The Big Weed"

When: Wednesday, March 12 (In-Service Day), noon – 1 p.m.

Where: High School Library

How: We will serve **a spectacular lunch buffet ready for you by 11:45 a.m.** As you arrive, please help yourself to a large plate of food and then take it to your assigned table, each one grouped by department. At each table, you'll find books arranged in order. Once you've marked a book using the classification system, simply place it on the cart next to your table.

- Place a red star on any book you think should be discarded.

- Place a green star on any book you think should be replaced.

- Place a gold star on all other books that you think we should keep.

- At the end, leave all the marked books on the table.

Don't worry—we know you'll have to make some difficult judgment calls, so rest assured, we will make the final decision on all discards.

Thanks for your help on this project!
The Library Team

Numerous studies have shown that careful weeding of a library collection will improve the quality, look, and feel of the collection by eliminating:

- Outdated books
- Worn, shabby, or damaged materials
- Inaccurate information

Some of the discarded books do not seem to fit the descriptions listed above, so why are perfectly good, up-to-date books being discarded?

The book in question may be:

- One of several duplicates
- At an inappropriate reading level for our population
- One that has not been checked out in the past five years
- Better suited to a classroom or other setting

Are you planning to eventually get rid of all print materials in the library?

The American Library Association has long advocated for librarians to support all informational formats to ensure we can properly serve our patrons' needs. If a particular format proves unreliable, is underused, or is not supported in the open market, then replacing it with newer, more efficient, and more effective technologies is recommended.

Time will tell whether or not print books will survive as a major format in the next decade. Personally, I believe we will still see print books produced but on a much smaller scale. Customer usage and the marketplace will probably be the determining factors. However, e-books will need to become lower in cost, provide enhanced features, and be much more user-friendly if they are to ever turn the tables on print.

Why do people like digital books? I prefer the hold, the look, and the feel of a real book.

Digital books are easier to store, easier to transport, and easier to access than print books. Enhanced digital books can provide information in many multimedia formats. Say, for example, you're a science student studying the heart. Wouldn't it be more powerful to see a real beating heart in the book you are reading? Additionally...

- Universal Access Digital Books are a specific type of e-book that provides access to an unlimited number of readers at the same time. This type of e-book is less common, but they are certainly worth looking for, as this is usually much less expensive than buying multiple print copies for a class.

- Digital books can be purchased and accessed within seconds, while it can take a library weeks or even months to offer access to new print books.

- Enhanced digital books are automatically updated on a much more regular basis as part of the library's overall purchase price.

What are the rules that go with the books you are giving teachers?

In a sense, there are no rules—we trust your professional judgment. If you want to claim the books as your personal copies and underline in them, go right ahead. If you want to make them part of your classroom library, by all means, do so. If you find the information in any of the books you've selected is inaccurate or outdated, we encourage you to discard the book so as not to pass the misinformation on to students and colleagues.

There is nothing more satisfying for a librarian or a reader than to be able to recommend just the right book for that person's needs. In a sense, a librarian can be a bibliotherapist or person who provides help with the right book at the right time. If you know the members of your faculty well, you can try this fun idea of recommending books which has worked well in our library.

BIBLIOTHERAPIST PRESCRIPTION

To: [Teacher's Name]

Using the tools of modern library science, our library team has developed a complex algorithm to determine your personality style, which we then matched with a book that we believe will rock your world.

As bibliotherapists, we do not want to prescribe what you read, but, instead, simply draw your attention to books you might enjoy or find useful. Feel free to keep this book, which has been checked out in your name, or simply take a brief look at it and then return it to the library or to Ron Starker's mailbox.

Disclaimer: Due to our position one degree north of the equator, our algorithm sometimes malfunctions. If this happens, we will order a new book title based on your recommendation and will loan it directly to you.

Oh, oh, oh, and please buy this book:

Title: _____

Author: _____

Sincerely,
The Library Team

CREATIVE MENTORS

If you work in a school library, consider recruiting students to become "creative mentors," who can help you think of ways to facilitate learning and use their energy, skills, and creativity to support their peers. My colleague, Paula Sivanandan, came up with the creative mentors concept as a spin-off of peer-to-peer tutoring. When we started our Creative Mentors club, we invited students to visit the library to learn how to use our studios. The idea was that once the students learned the basics, they could try projects that interested them, recruit their friends to get involved in the projects, and then teach those students how to use the tools and facilities.

This year, we limited the club's enrollment to ten students per grade level (sixth, seventh, and eighth grades), which has allowed us to work one-on-one with each student and properly share limited materials, equipment, and working space. We meet weekly and offer workshops from time to time on such topics such as:

- Making string instruments
- Creating videos using iMovie
- Creating avatars using CrazyTalk Animator
- 3-D printing basics
- Kite building
- Making model planes, cars, boats, etc.
- Basic photography skills using iPads
- Coding with Sphero
- Using VR programs and Google Cardboard viewers
- Building 3-D paper objects
- Bodily-kinesthetic workshop using hoverboards, unicycles, rip sticks, balance beams, etc.
- Construction using LEGO bricks and Keva Planks
- Group drumming and team building

We plan to video each workshop and make it available to students not in the club so they can try the activity on their own and come to the library for help. The club's goal is to encourage students to share skills with their peers, who can then design their own projects. This approach has been highly successful, resulting in an amazing number of student projects that they are choosing to do without credit or as part of a class. Our next step is to try to further integrate this service with the work teachers are doing so as to better support the curriculum. Nevertheless, we will still provide help to students or faculty on projects that interest them, regardless of whether it fits within the curriculum or not. Our aim is not only to support the curriculum but also to personalize education and essentially expand the curriculum.

Another approach to this type of club could include badges, certificates, and requiring students to go through a kind of boot camp on how to problem solve and how to help others in the classroom. As students meet the requirements, you could provide a list of qualified creative mentors to teachers, who could then be called upon to help with project-based learning assignments.

Library Survival Kit

Once you've tried some of the ideas I've mentioned, or better yet, tried ideas designed to your community's specific needs, ask your library's members for feedback: How do they like the changes? How could you improve? What types of services or physical changes would they like to see in the library?

You could easily ask these questions in the form of a survey online using tools such as SurveyMonkey, Zoho, or Google Forms. For more inspiration, read "7 Best Survey Tools: Create Awesome Surveys for Free!" here: bit.ly/2hXaYHa.

The Moonshot: No Fear

If your goal is to eventually build an incredible hybrid library that incorporates all the best innovative thinking, resources, staff, and passion, then you're engaging in "Moonshot Thinking," as depicted in the YouTube video with the same name. Moonshot thinking is the idea that sometimes we need to take bold steps in the same manner that John F. Kennedy set America on a path to go to the moon. The idea of Moonshot Thinking is to show no fear, to take a calculated risk, and go for a big change.

CHAPTER 24

Designing the Future

The best way to predict the future is to design it.
—*Buckminster Fuller*

The future ain't what it used to be.
—*Yogi Berra*

Hey, congratulations! You've almost finished this book ...
or maybe you just skipped ahead. Whatever the case, I'm just
happy you didn't fling it into the fireplace or pool.

If you haven't noticed, my approach has not been overly scholarly;
I'm a practitioner, not a theorist. Theorists are important—they illuminate new areas and shine light down long tunnels to guide us in a logical direction—but it is the practitioners who are walking the walk and making the journey through unpredictable circumstances with unpredictable customers making unpredictable demands. We can't always talk our way out of situations—we have to come up with solutions. We have to directly engage in a creative, innovative fashion, even when a pack of "screenagers" is coming our way.

Having established that, I have a small confession: At least 50 percent of the information in this book may be wrong in the near future.

No, you cannot have your money back. I never promised to be an expert. I simply stated I have worked as a librarian for a long time, I've read a kajillion articles and talked to people far more intelligent than myself in an effort to provide you with some good ideas and some good information. Experts in the field may be able to do better, but I'm guessing they would also be wrong on many counts.

You see, it all goes back to a lecture I heard while attending Lewis & Clark College. John Richards, PhD, one of my favorite professors, said, "At least 50 percent of what we are teaching you at this college is probably wrong; the trouble is we don't know which 50 percent." When I questioned him as to whether or not we'd get 50 percent of our tuition returned, he said that wasn't in the cards. So, you see, I'm simply following his method.

Predicting the future is a difficult, albeit worthy, activity. We need to take a close look at our trajectory and see where we're going so we can avoid the big obstacles in our path. We can look ahead a year or two with considerable accuracy, but like a car on the highway, our headlights and vision only allow us to see so far into the darkness of uncertainty.

We shape our tools and then our tools shape us.
—*Father John Culkin*

THE MEDIUM IS THE MESSAGE

In *The Medium is the Massage* (a typo that McLuhan spotted and decided to keep) McLuhan discusses the interaction between language and thinking and how, depending upon the transmission device, words can result in different interpretations and meanings. For example, words transmitted in print come across differently than spoken words, which are, in turn, received differently than words in videos. His famous quote sounds very much like a remix of what John Culkin originally said, yet was credited to Winston Churchill when he uttered just a few years earlier: "We shape our buildings; thereafter, they shape us." Culkin's words were made famous by Churchill and later by McLuhan when he changed the medium from buildings to tools. Our culture's transmission cables are represented through face-to-face conversations, phone calls, books, recordings, art, graphics, films, videos, websites, tweets, Instagram messages, and other mediums, many of which didn't exist when McLuhan was alive.

Predicting the future of education is far more challenging than in many other areas, as education is at the very intersection of community norms, politics, economics, technological developments, health factors, crime rates, human development, and family involvement. But several organizations are trying to do just this, among them the Association of American Colleges & Universities, the Center for Public Education, EDUCAUSE, the International Society for Technology in Education, KnowledgeWorks, the Metiri Group, the Organisation for Economic Co-operation and Development, and the Partnership for 21st Century Learning.

KnowledgeWorks has provided a leading role in tracking future educational trends. "KnowledgeWorks explores the future of learning to help education leaders and innovators anticipate change, explore strategic possibilities, and identify ways of creating better opportunities for all learners."

KnowledgeWorks presented a learning scenario for year 2025 with four possible futures. Two of these futures focus on the prosumer and two on the provider.

In the first scenario, learning becomes personalized to the extent that learners create their own "'personal learning ecologies' by selecting from a range of learning settings." This scenario fits fairly well with my vision for school libraries.

The ALA's Center for the Future of Libraries is an excellent resource to check out if you're interested in learning about the issues librarians will be facing. I recommend going to the "Trends" section, which organizes trends into seven categories ("STEEPED"): "Society," "Technology," "Education," "Environment," "Politics (and Government)," "Economics," and "Demographics."

These topics provide insights into the ALA's perspective on the future and offer some great ideas for how libraries can adapt:

- **Aging Advances**: Life expectancy is rising and populations are growing older.

- **Anonymity**: Libraries and librarians are strong advocates for personal privacy and for the protection of patrons from probes into their reading habits by outside individuals or groups.

- **Badging**: Recognize the achievement of specific skills using this form of micro-credentialing.

- **Collective Impact**: Align common agendas, shared measurement systems, mutually reinforcing activities, and continuous communication.

- **Connected Learning**: Use digital and social media to create peer-supported learning environments.

- **Data Everywhere**: Data is being increasingly collected through the Internet of things.

- **Digital Natives**: There are huge generational differences between younger individuals, who are often referred to as "digital natives" because they have grown up with digital technology, and older "digital immigrants" who adopted these skills and practices later in life.

- **Drones**: Drones provide new opportunities for content creation and research.

- **Emerging Adulthood**: Individuals in their late teens and early twenties are taking longer to leave home and settle into careers.

- **Fandom**: This is a community of people who are passionate about something, whether it's a film, band, television show, book, or sports team.

- **Fast Casual**: Individuals are seeking more active, social spaces with experiential value.

- **Flipped Learning**: Students are provided lessons online, allowing class time to be spent working through and solving questions together.

- **Gamification**: Libraries are increasingly promoting games and game-based learning.

- **Haptic Technology**: This wearable technology can be used to search and navigate library spaces.

- **Income Inequality**: Libraries can help bridge the income-inequality gap by providing educational resources otherwise unavailable to low-income groups.

- **Internet of Things**: As more and more data is collected by devices around us, libraries may be involved in handling new informational sources that reveal trends and patterns.

- **Maker Movement**: Libraries are beginning to provide their members with opportunities to create content for personal, community, and library use.

- **Privacy Shifting**: The way we view privacy is going through dramatic changes, and libraries can play an important role in shaping policies and practices.

- **Resilience**: As libraries are called upon to provide assistance in disaster situations, they can help individuals cope through resilient practices.

- **Robots**: Libraries will tap robots' potential for facilitating learning alongside human beings.

- **Sharing Economy**: Along with sharing resources, learning spaces, and books, more libraries will also be sharing physical tools and skills.

- **Unplugged**: By rebranding quiet spaces into unplugged areas or "Walden Zones," libraries can offer members a break from the constant bombardment of technology.

- **Urbanization**: Libraries may have to adapt to new usage patterns and needs as our populations become more urbanized.

FOLLOWING THE CURVE

Each year, Gartner, Inc., a leading information technology research company, produces its "Hype Cycle for Emerging Technologies," offering us a fascinating look at emerging technologies and their position in the adoption cycle. The Gartner curve allows us to visualize which technologies are just getting started, which ones are just reaching the peak of their expectations, which are entering the natural drop in expectations, and which ones are gaining productivity. It has proved fairly reliable and can be a useful tool for us to reference when determining which technologies we should incorporate into our libraries.

According to Gartner's "Hype Cycle for Emerging Technologies," these three key areas will affect the world of technology:

- **Transparently immersive experiences**: 4-D printing, brain-computer interfacing, human augmentation, volumetric displays, affective computing, connected homes, nanotube electronics, AR, VR, and gesture-controlled devices

- **The perceptual smart machine age with the following key developments**: Smart dust, machine learning, virtual personal assistants, cognitive expert advisors, smart data discovery, smart workspaces, conversational user interfaces, smart robots, commercial UAVs (drones), autonomous vehicles, natural-language question answering, personal analytics, enterprise taxonomy and ontology management, Data Broker PaaS (dbrPaaS), and context brokering

- **Key, platform-enabling technologies**: Neuromorphic hardware, quantum computing, Blockchain, IoT Platform, software-defined security, and software-defined anything (SDx)

Will these emerging technologies have a significant effect on libraries? Will we use tools for human augmentation, personal learning assistants, or quantum computing in the libraries of the future? As librarians, we need to be aware of these new and emerging technologies so we can make informed decisions about our libraries' futures.

The annual *Horizon Report*, published by the New Media Consortium (NMC) and the Consortium for School Networking (CoSN), has been a highly valuable resource for my colleagues and me during the past several years. In fact, the K–12, Library, Museum, and Higher Ed editions have helped guide us in our work.

Here is a sampling from the Horizon Report 2016 K–12 edition:

Near Term (one year or less)

Trends: Coding as a literacy and students as creators
Developments in Technology: Maker spaces and online learning

Mid-Term (two to three years)

Trends: Collaborative learning and deeper learning approaches
Developments in Technology: Robotics and VR

Far Term (four to five years)

Trends: Redesigning learning spaces and rethinking how schools work
Developments in Technology: Stay tuned! *The Horizon Report* is produced by university academics, as well as industry innovators

who examine and evaluate the most promising technologies being introduced in schools, universities, libraries, and museums for their impact on learning. It is the best single source I know of for keeping abreast of developments with new emerging technologies and their applications within educational settings.

CHAPTER 25

Paradigm Shift

End with a bang, not a whimper.
                        —Veronica Campbell,
        my English teacher at Umatilla High School

M y high school English teacher, Veronica Campbell, once wrote at the end of one of my essays, "End with a bang, not a whimper," and then she wrote, "corruption of T.S. Eliot."

> *This is the way the world ends*
> *This is the way the world ends*
> *This is the way the world ends*
> *Not with a bang but a whimper.*
>   *—T.S. Eliot, "The Hollow Men"*

I had no idea what she was talking about, but she explained to me that she was turning the last line of Eliot's poem "The Hollow Men" into a counter-directive: wake the reader up, deliver a bang, agitate, reignite the spark, bring home the bacon, and deliver the goods (or something like that), but don't end your writing in a whimper. Okay, Veronica, this chapter is dedicated to you.

Know the rules well, so you can break them effectively.
—*Dalai Lama XIV*

Learn the rules like a pro,
so you can break them like an artist.
—*Pablo Picasso*

Old-fashioned libraries are often associated with rules. Lots of rules. We have some rules posted in our library that are just for fun.

"Velociraptor-Free Zone."

While there aren't any clear rules for how our libraries should change in the future, I have picked up a few that I think could be helpful. (See "Toolkit of Library Rules" on page 240.)

PEANUTS, POPCORN, PARADIGMS!

As you continually seek better ways to facilitate your members' learning, remember this: you alone are not responsible for changing the entire educational system, but you can be a catalyst for positive change.

There is room for more than one paradigm, room for more than one type of library, and room for more than one type of librarian. In the coming years, we'll need flexible, agile minds to take control and take the initiative in dealing with the forces of globalization, the information explosion, digitization, and the profound knowledge acceleration.

A MULTIPLE-INTELLIGENCES APPROACH IS NOT THE ONLY ANSWER

My colleagues and I decided to use Howard Gardner's theory of multiple intelligences as an organizational structure and method for reminding us about all the forms of learning we want to support in our library. We don't worry about determining if a student project falls into the category of spatial or logical/mathematical intelligence; most learning activities involve more than one type of intelligence in the process anyway. Instead, these intelligences offer us an opportunity to see what we're missing.

For example, by having a wellness studio, we're reminded, "Oh, yeah, by paying attention to their personal wellness, students will be happier, more effective learners." As librarians, we need to find ways to foster this kind of thinking. My library's learning design studios for musical, spatial, and linguistic intelligence all remind us of our mission: "To facilitate learning and knowledge creation. We will assist members in becoming thoughtful users and creators of information, with an emphasis on improving society through lifelong learning."

TOOLKIT OF LIBRARY RULES
(Well, actually, just ideas to consider)

- Avoid ideology. Stay neutral and flexible—there are many ways to learn.
- Remember, culture eats strategy, so learn to understand the culture.
- Make your library a playground of learning and discovery.
- Facilitate learning using each of the multiple intelligences.
- Make your library feel like home—inviting and comfortable.
- Everything is connected, so connect the dots for better understanding.
- Create zones ranging from quiet and reflective to active and collaborative.
- Consult students and stakeholders frequently.
- Make the library a hub for learning and entertainment.
- De-institutionalize schools and libraries whenever possible.
- Realize libraries have no boundaries when it comes to learning.
- Upcycle materials and ideas.
- Curate the best of everything.
- Seek to understand your local community's needs and then help facilitate and implement innovative solutions.
- Open the ideas in your books and make them visible.
- Provide opportunities for service to others.
- Build your collection based on your library members' needs.
- Eagerly support reading.
- Give equal attention to all forms of learning, not just reading.
- Promote awareness about global issues, such as climate change.
- Help library members pursue their passions.
- Trigger the senses: iHear, iSee, iFeel, iTaste, and iSmell.

TOOLKIT OF LIBRARY RULES (CONT.)

- Display student work and make learning visible.
- Ensure the library is a safe haven for everyone.
- Encourage your patrons to add information and resources to the library.
- Try one radical idea and get stakeholder feedback.
- Examine each zone to identify areas needing improvement.
- Support lifelong learning, a luxury libraries can afford to consider.
- Establish the library as the testing ground for new hardware, software, and pedagogy.
- First, above all, do no harm (Latin: Primum non nocere).
- Make use of natural light and experiment with other forms of lighting.
- Design flexible and agile spaces.
- When necessary, create purpose-built areas.
- Avoid built-in shelving and furniture.
- Constantly discover the joy in learning and pass it on to others.
- Create an awareness of nature through plants and animals.
- Consider the needs of introverts and extroverts.
- Provide opportunities for hands-on learning.
- Promote health and wellness.
- Learn about learning and then apply what you learn.
- Think laterally (reverse it, flip it, magnify it, shrink it).
- Remix—copy, transform, and combine.
- Libraries are often too serious; adopt a good sense of humor to be more approachable to students.
- Stop asking for permission, and instead, simply exercise good judgment.

LONG LIVE THE REVOLUTION

The days of the timid, reclusive librarian are over. Since we aren't seen as revolutionaries, we have the perfect cover for covertly leading a revolution. In 1974, only a rabid anti-communist, like Richard Nixon, could negotiate diplomatic relations with communist China, and in the same vein, only school librarians have the latitude it will take to lead an educational revolution. After all, who would suspect that the mild-mannered, rule-abiding, by-the-book (no pun intended) librarian would actually be leading a revolution for change within your school?

Episode of the Belgian Revolution of 1830 by Gustaf Wappers, 1834

School administrators are the last ones to rely upon to make radical changes in education. Don't get me wrong, I have many friends who are school administrators, and they are intelligent, hardworking, dedicated individuals who want good things to happen in their schools. Generally speaking, however, administrators are the standard bearers of the status quo. They are often mired in the relentless "edubabble" sold to us through successive waves of curriculum and textbook publishers.

And some, feel as if they have, more or less, reached the pinnacle of their careers (and are finally earning decent salaries) because they've learned not to rock the boat. Why take major risks when there is so much to lose?

No, the revolution rests on our shoulders. Now, I'm not talking about running around with guns and explosives; rather, the revolution I am proposing is a nonviolent one and involves changing the system from within.

Libraries usually occupy a sizable footprint in a school's physical structure. It is all too tempting for schools to consider completely digitizing libraries and converting the physical structure into more classrooms. (In private, tuition-paying schools, and even in public schools that receive state money based on average daily attendance, more classrooms mean more money.) To survive this kind of thinking, school libraries need to offer resources, spaces, and services that are not available in the classroom.

The library is the one place within a school, and sometimes even within a community, that can operate with some degree of independence from the status quo. Libraries have the potential to break out of the relentless grind of lockstep educational tradition, rigid schedules, departmentalization, standardization, Common Core, and overall bureaucratization of the educational practice. Libraries offer their patrons a chance to breathe again, to think for themselves, to conduct independent research and investigation, and to create and explore beyond the boundaries of the prescribed curriculum.

If you are a teacher, you may be thinking, "This guy has no idea what he is talking about. I haven't drunk the Kool-Aid—I'm leading my own revolution within my classroom." I suspect our best teachers are all following their consciences, trying the most effective ideas in teaching their students and pretending compliance with the system while conducting a soft revolution. I am simply advocating for libraries to better support teachers' work with spaces, resources, and people.

This revolution embraces a diversity of viewpoints and approaches, rather than one dogma and doctrine.

Schools usually greet change through the introduction of a new administration working in conjunction with a school board to reshape and redirect education, so as to better meet the students' and families'

TOOLKIT OF ALTERNATIVE POINTS OF VIEW TO CONSIDER

- **The Geography of Genius:** This book looks at where learning can occur and captures their best ideas.

- **Human performance:** Focus on human growth, life-span development, and lifelong learning through positive psychology and wellness approaches.

- **Learning commons:** Make the library a place where patrons can experience something by incorporating science centers, museums, media labs, and so on.

- **Science museum models:** Use a STEAM model along with exploratoriums, technology museums, innovation centers, etc.

- **Service-learning models:** This is my favorite, as it addresses authentic learning and social problems in an organic, meaningful way.

- **Taxonomy-based:** Involve your library in curating each academic discipline's taxonomies and then incorporating those approaches into support.

- **Trigger the senses:** Focus learning on extensions of our senses using iSense: iSee, iHear, iTaste, iSmell, and iFeel.

needs. The new administration's motives are good and pure, to be sure, but the results are often the same: the superintendent launches a strategic plan and committees are formed. Teachers seeking to become administrators jump on the bandwagon and accept unpaid leadership positions. Overworked teachers hastily develop new curriculum using what little time they have during their regular day. Committees make compromises; reports are written (and often simply scanned, as no one has the time for reflection and analysis); and the whole thing rolls out way too soon, usually without proper training or professional development. An educational guru or two (or three) may be brought in, but their effects are minimal, since culture eats strategy and change has to happen from within. The new educational model is unveiled with great fanfare with highly polished graphics, charts and data, but in the classroom, life looks pretty much the same. Teachers tick the boxes and carry on as best they can, day in and day out.

Education is a difficult, complex business, in part, because we don't fully understand how students learn, nor do we know how to properly assess and measure their comprehension of the content. We still have a lot to learn about how to address people's individual differences and employ models, such as Gardner's forms of intelligence, so we can better engage our students. This is not to say we should give up; rather, I think we need to take a different approach.

Universities teaching library and information science, in general, are not training future librarians how to be radicals. No, we librarians are the standard bearers of the system, the monks within the church of doctrine. Traditional librarians are often drawn to the profession to retreat from the rough-and-tumble world of classrooms and unruly students. They embrace regular education the way a monk embraces the gospel—not through radical action but through contemplative reflection. Too often, librarians are introverted, former English teachers, hoping to find solace in literature and seeking to build a joyful heaven, where only books beg for their attention. But the fact that you've read this book to the end suggests you may not be a traditional librarian at all. In fact, I suspect you may be a fellow radical operating like a ninja without fanfare.

For those of you who are traditional librarians, it is nice work if you can get it, but the days of the traditional library are soon coming to an end. The church—I mean, school—demands higher productivity, higher accountability, and higher value.

A dynamic library with well-curated resources, innovative facilities, administrative support, and, most importantly, a talented staff of academic coaches and technicians can serve as a catalyst for change in our schools and in our communities. Don't create a separate innovation center in your school or city. Instead, incorporate your innovation center into the library. Why? Because libraries have a long history of protecting freedom of information, they have established norms for encouraging all points of view, and they are not bound totally by a specific curriculum, doctrine, or a special interest group. Libraries have always catered to individualized and personalized education and they have always embraced new ideas and new technologies. Consider the possibility that in this highly complex and radically changing world that we live in, libraries might serve as centers of innovation, providing a means for individuals from all walks of life to design creative solutions to our challenging and exciting future.

Bibliography

Future Libraries: Workshops Summary and Emerging Insights. Arup University, July 2015.

Asimov, Isaac. *I, Robot.* New York: Bantam, 2004.

Bell, C. Gordon, and Jim Gemmell. *Total Recall: How the E-Memory Revolution Will Change Everything.* New York: Dutton, 2009.

Buzan, Tony, and Susanna Abbott. *The Ultimate Book of Mind Maps: Unlock Your Creativity, Boost Your Memory, Change Your Life.* London: Harper Collins, 2005.

Cain, Susan. *Quiet: The Power of Introverts in a World That Can't Stop Talking.* New York: Crown, 2012.

Campbell, James W. P., and Will Pryce. *The Library: A World History.* London: Thames & Hudson, 2013.

Crawford, Matthew B. *Shop Class as Soulcraft: An Inquiry into the Value of Work.* New York: Penguin, 2009.

Davidson, Cathy, David Goldberg, and Zoë Marie Jones. *The Future of Learning Institutions in a Digital Age.* MIT Press, 2009. bit.ly/2n9NZLH.

Dickens, Charles. *A Tale of Two Cities*, adapted by Marian Leighton. New York, NY: Baronet, 1992.

Eisenberg, Michael, Carrie A. Lowe, and Kathleen L. Spitzer. *Information Literacy: Essential Skills for the Information Age.* Westport, CT: Libraries Unlimited, 2004.

Friedman, Thomas L. *The World Is Flat: A Brief History of the Twenty-First Century.* New York: Farrar, Straus and Giroux, 2005.

Fuller, R. Buckminster. *Critical Path.* New York: St. Martin's, 1981.

Future Libraries: Workshops Summary and Emerging Insights. London: Arup University, July 2015.

Gaiman, Neil. *The View from the Cheap Seats: Selected Nonfiction.* New York: William Morrow, 2016.

Gardner, Howard. *Frames of Mind: The Theory of Multiple Intelligences.* New York: Basic, 1983.

Gladwell, Malcolm. *The Tipping Point: How Little Things Can Make a Big Difference.* Boston: Little, Brown, 2000.

Goleman, Daniel. *Emotional Intelligence: Why It Can Matter More than IQ.* London: Bloomsbury, 2004.

Greenfield, Susan. *Mind Change: How Digital Technologies Are Leaving Their Mark on Our Brains.* New York: Random House, 2015.

Hattie, John. *Visible Learning: A Synthesis of over 800 Meta-Analyses Relating to Achievement.* London: Routledge, 2009.

Hirsch, E. D., Joseph F. Kett, and James Trefil. *Cultural Literacy: What Every American Needs to Know.* Boston: Houghton Mifflin, 1987.

Hokusai, Katsushika. "The Great Wave off Kanagawa"

Horowitz, Alexandra. *On Looking: Eleven Walks with Expert Eyes.* New York: Scriber, 2013.

IBM Global Technology Services. "The Toxic Terabyte: How Data-Dumping Threatens Business Efficiency," July 2006.

Information Power: Building Partnerships for Learning. Chicago: American Library Association, 1998.

Jimb0. "Analog vs. Digital." *SparkFun.* learn.sparkfun.com/tutorials/analog-vs-digital.

Johnson, Steven. "Where Good Ideas Come From." *TED Talk,* June 2010 ted.com/talks/steven_johnson_where_good_ideas_come_from.

Jones, William P. *Keeping Found Things Found: The Study and Practice of Personal Information Management*. Amsterdam: Morgan Kaufmann, 2008.

Kaye, Cathryn Berger. *The Complete Guide to Service Learning: Proven, Practical Ways to Engage Students in Civic Responsibility, Academic Curriculum, & Social Action*. Minneapolis: Free Spirit Pub., 2004.

Kelley, David, and Tom Kelley. *Creative Confidence: Unleashing the Creative Potential within Us All*. New York: Crown Business, 2013.

Kelly, Kevin. *Cool Tools: A Catalog of Possibilities*. Hong Kong: Cool Tools Lab, 2013.

Kelly, Kevin. *The Inevitable: Understanding the 12 Technological Forces That Will Shape Our Future*. New York: Viking, 2016.

Kennedy, George. *The Cambridge History of Literary Criticism: Classical Criticism*. New York: University of Cambridge Press, 1999.

Krueger, Keith. "Learning to Change—Changing to Learn." YouTube, May 15, 2008. bit.ly/2h4PiIw.

Kurzweil, Ray. *The Singularity Is Near*. London: Duckworth, 2006.

Lacey, Sharon. "Is the Library the New Public Square?" Arts MIT, March 22, 2016. arts.mit.edu/library-new-public-square.

Lankes, R. David. *The Atlas of New Librarianship*. Cambridge, NJ: MIT Press, 2011.

Lankes, R. David. *Expect More: Demanding Better Libraries for Today's Complex World*. 2012.

Larsson, Thomas. *The Race to the Top: The Real Story of Globalization*. Washington, D.C.: CATO Institute, 2003.

Lerner, Fred. *Story of Libraries: From the Invention of Writing to the Computer Age*. London: Continuum, 2009.

Lippman, Peter C. *Evidence-Based Design of Elementary and Secondary Schools*. Hoboken, NJ: J. Wiley, 2010.

Moore, Perry. *Hero*. New York: Disney-Hyperion, 2009.

McLeod, Saul. "Erik Erickson." *Simply Psychology*. 2008, 2017. simplypsychology.org/Erik-Erikson.html

Medina, John. *Brain Rules: 12 Principles for Surviving and Thriving at Work, Home, and School*. Seattle: Pear, 2008.

Nair, Prakash, and Randall Fielding. *The Language of School Design: Design Patterns for 21st Century Schools*. Minneapolis: DesignShare, 2005.

"Selected Statistics From the Public Elementary and Secondary Education Universe: School Year 2014–15." National Center for Education Statistics, Institute of Education Sciences, September 2016. nces.ed.gov/pubs2016/2016076.pdf.

Peresie, Michelle; Linda B. Alexander. "Librarian stereotypes in Young Adult literature". *Young Adult Library Services*, Fall 2005.

Pink, Daniel H. *A Whole New Mind: Moving from the Information Age to the Conceptual Age*. New York: Riverhead, 2005.

Randles, Clint. "Why music lessons need to keep up with the times." *The Conversation*, June 2, 2016. theconversation.com/why-music-lessons-need-to-keep-up-with-the-times-58268.

"Ratey, John J., and Eric Hagerman. *Spark: The Revolutionary New Science of Exercise and the Brain*. New York: Little, Brown, 2008.

Ritchhart, Ron, Mark Church, and Karin Morrison. *Making Thinking Visible: How to Promote Student Engagement, Understanding, and Independence*. San Francisco: Jossey-Bass, 2011.

Rosenbaum, Steven C. *Curation Nation: Why the Future of Content Is Context: How to Win in a World Where Consumers Are Creators*. New York: McGraw-Hill, 2011.

Samples, Bob. *The Metaphoric Mind: A Celebration of Creative Consciousness.* Reading, MA: Addison-Wesley Pub., 1976.

Shirky, Clay. *Cognitive Surplus: Creativity and Generosity in a Connected Age.* New York: Penguin, 2010.

Siegler, MG. "Eric Schmidt: Every 2 Days We Create As Much Information As We Did Up To 2003." *Tech Crunch*, August 4, 2010. techcrunch.com/2010/08/04/schmidt-data.

Sinek, Simon. "How Great Leaders Inspire Action." *TED Talk*, September 2009. ted.com/talks/simon_sinek_how_great _leaders_inspire_action.

Sunstein, Cass R., Sean Pratt, and Richard H. Thaler. *Nudge: Improving Decisions About Health, Wealth, and Happiness.* New York: Penguin Books, 2014.

Templar, Richard. *The Rules of Life: A Personal Code for Living a Better, Happier, More Successful Life.* Upper Saddle River, NJ: Pearson Prentice Hall, 2006.

The Third Teacher: 79 Ways You Can Use Design to Transform Teaching & Learning. New York: Abrams, 2010.

Toffler, Alvin. *The Third Wave.* New York: Morrow, 1980.

Trumble, Kelly, and Robina MacIntyre Marshall. *The Library of Alexandria.* New York: Clarion, 2003.

Waters, Richard. "Valley Visitors must Bring Back more than T-Shirts," *The Financial Times.* April 18, 2013.

Wesch, Michael. "A Vision of Students Today." *Wimp.com.* wimp. com/a-vision-of-students-today.

Wolf, Maryanne. *Proust and the Squid: The Story and Science of the Reading Brain.* New York: Harper Perennial, 2008.

Woodford, Chris. "Analog and digital." *Explain That Stuff.* March 3, 2017. www.explainthatstuff.com/analog-and-digital.html.

Zhao, Yong. *World Class Learners: Educating Creative and Entrepreneurial Students.* Thousand Oaks, CA: Corwin, 2012.

Photo Credits

Katsushika Hokusai, *The Great Wave of Kanagawa*, color woodblock, ca. 1829–1833, bit.ly/2oKxaJh.

Takasunrise0921, *The British Library*, Wikimedia, Creative Commons 2.5, December 4, 2005, bit.ly/2hzApiL.

Lydia May, *1st time delving into the digital world*, May 9, 2015, bit.ly/2hHPqPh.

Eric E. Castro, *Margerie Glacier & Mt Fairweather*, Wikimedia, Creative Commons 2.0, July 17, 2010, bit.ly/2hwnb5k.

Great Images in NASA, *Space Shuttle Columbia Launching*, Wikimedia, Creative Commons, public domain, April 12, 1981, bit.ly/2oUTD4X.

O. Von Corven, *The Great Library of Alexandria*, 19th Century, Wikimedia Commons, bit.ly/2hI0fAB.

Carsten Whimster, *The Bibliotheca Alexandrina from the Mediterranean side*, Wikimedia Creative Commons 3.0, October 28, 2006, bit.ly/2r5T5aB

The Opte Project, *Internet Map 1024*, Wikimedia, Creative Commons 2.5, bit.ly/2hj5qCM

Shahrin Aripin, *Library Zones*, bit.ly/2oHUiUx

Doug Tindal, *Hollywood Stars*, Christian Haugen, Hollywood, Sandy Innes-Hill as Harry Potter and Patrick Green as Uncle Sam Photo by Doug Tindal, bit.ly/2oX1T1P.

Shahrin Aripin, *Papercrafts 4*, April 24, 2017, bit.ly/2qhibq2.

Jeff Koltutsky, *Koltutsky Tiger*, bit.ly/2puGn3O

Shahrin Aripin, *Oculus Rift 3*, bit.ly/2pvya43.

Egide Charles Gustave, Baron Wappers, *Episode of the Belgian Revolution of 1830,* Szilas at the Royal Museums of Fine Arts of Belgium, Brussels, Wikipedia, public domain, December 31, 1834, bit.ly/2ipF6sJ.

Toolkit Resources

Introduction

Terri Rolfe: "AIS Vienna Library Orientation" video — *bit.ly/2h9VAbj*

The Road to Shambhala, Osho News Online Magazine — *bit.ly/2nEwyR5*

Singapore American School Middle School Library — *bit.ly/2hXvPaK*

Garrison Keillor — *bit.ly/2h9UFHX*

Chapter 1: The Best of Times

A Tale of Two Cities — *amzn.to/2hXGJ0m*

The Library: A World History — *amzn.to/2i7Mo7y*

Library of Congress — *bit.ly/2ha4hCE*

British Library — *bit.ly/2hFjFFV*

American Library Association (ALA) Fact Sheet — *bit.ly/2idaKlV*

Online Computer Library Center U.S. Statistics: — *bit.ly/2hSzlq4*

ALA Careers — *bit.ly/2hRg1qp*

U.S. News & World Report, Library School Rankings — *bit.ly/2hoKTOc*

Top-Rated Graduate Programs in Library and Information Studies

Archives and Preservation	*bit.ly/2i1LOat*
Digital Librarianship	*bit.ly/2ic0NPI*
Health Librarianship	*bit.ly/2i1O4yw*
Information Systems	*bit.ly/2i9lJEm*
Law Librarianship	*bit.ly/2hszbq0*
School Library Media	*bit.ly/2i9mPA5*
Services for Children and Youth	*bit.ly/2hszsJv*
Google Books Library Project	*bit.ly/2h7PfLT*
The Third Wave	*amzn.to/2id3LQI*
Buckminster Fuller	*bit.ly/2hRjXYz*
The Atlas of New Librarianship	*amzn.to/2gZlA39*

Toolkit for Research on Libraries

Association of College & Research Libraries (ACRL)	*bit.ly/2ha24ak*
Directory of Public Libraries: Libraries.org	*bit.ly/2ha55aA*
OCLC's Global Library Statistics	*bit.ly/2hSzlq4*
Pew Research Center	*pewrsr.ch/2h80hAK*

The Universal Digital Library   *bit.ly/2hXCMsv*

U.S. Institute of Museum and Library Services   *bit.ly/2hafm6v*

Chapter 2: The Perfect Storm

The Perfect Storm video clip   *bit.ly/2idgodT*

Center for Generational Kinetics: "Generational   *bit.ly/2gZZsH3*
Breakdown"
Lydia: "1st Time Delving into the Digital World"   *bit.ly/2hHPqPh*

"The Top Six Library Issues"   *bit.ly/2hXWJ2r*

The World Is Flat   *amzn.to/2hXTGap*

The Race to the Top   *amzn.to/2hahwDh*

Critical Path   *amzn.to/2hahSK7*

"The Toxic Terabyte"   *Ibm.co/2gZZvT4*

"Every 2 Days"   *tcrn.ch/2hp2vcU*

"Three Laws of Robotics"   *bit.ly/2hSRGTR*

The Singularity Is Near   *bit.ly/2I9QPQf*

Chapter 3: Everything Is a Remix, Even This Title

"Everything Is a Remix"   *bit.ly/2h02Sth*

"Library of Alexandria"   *bit.ly/2hanyDV*

The Third Teacher   *amzn.to/2havaGx*

The Library of Alexandria   *amzn.to/2hSZvJa*

The Library of Alexandria   *amzn.to/2hSZvJa*

ALA: *Standards for the 21st-Century Learner*   *bit.ly/2haFJZY*

Chapter 4: That's So Yesterday

ALA: Information Power   *bit.ly/2hFZaJ9*

ALA: Standards for the 21st-Century Learner   *bit.ly/2haFJZY*

"How Great Leaders Inspire Action"   *bit.ly/2hpdGSM*

Eight Signs of Intelligence   *bit.ly/2haB8a8*

The Atlas of New Librarianship   *amzn.to/2gZIA39*

The Future of Learning Institutions in a Digital Age   *bit.ly/2n9NZLH*

Chapter 5: Censored

Banned Books Week   *bit.ly/2hTu7tP*

Library Bill of Rights   *bit.ly/2h0BcEp*

Challenge Support   *bit.ly/2hTvlp9*

Hero	*amzn.to/2rDc2l1*
Reconsideration of Library Resources	*bit.ly/2h0mBJo*

Toolkit of Resources for Book and Material Challenges

Challenge Support	*bit.ly/2hShKMm*
Challenged Materials	*bit.ly/2hGqyXM*
Checklist and Ideas for Library Staff Working with Community Leaders	*bit.ly/2hTvHMi*
Code of Ethics	*bit.ly/2hb5UQd*
Coping with Challenges	*bit.ly/2h8HPrC*
Core Values of Librarianship	*bit.ly/2hGgtdg*
Developing a Confidentiality Policy	*bit.ly/2ie6Gbv*
Developing Public Library Internet Use Policy	*bit.ly/2hGrHi1*
Freedom to Read	*bit.ly/2hpN4kG*
Freedom to View Statement	*bit.ly/2hpFdDC*
Interpretations of the Library Bill of Rights	*bit.ly/2hpKYkE*
Libraries: An American Value	*bit.ly/2i8OF2k*
Library Bill of Rights	*bit.ly/2h0BcEp*

Chapter 6: Where's Wally? Accessing Info

Google Books Library Project	*bit.ly/2idZj3A*
Google Guide	*bit.ly/2hZ4y7Z*
TNW: "30 Specialized Search Engines"	*bit.ly/2hpVMzp*
Plagiarism Today: "Finding the Age of a Page"	*bit.ly/2hbbL8o*
MIT: "How to Carbon-Date a Web Page"	*bit.ly/2i8UZ9X*
Ask Leo!: "How Do I Find out When a Web Page Was Written?"	*bit.ly/2hSpaPK*
9to5 Google	*bit.ly/2h0Fiwz*
HubSpot: "Tips & Tricks for Searching Google Like a Pro"	*bit.ly/2hTHB95*
"Google Algorithm Change History"	*bit.ly/2hZ8FRn*
Moz: "Keyword Explorer"	*bit.ly/2i8Ugpg*
Search Engine Land: "Google: Algorithm Updates"	*selnd.com/2h8SpyU*
Search Engine Watch	*bit.ly/2ie3TPh*
"Dark web"	*bit.ly/2hZ4PaZ*
"World Wide Web"	*bit.ly/2hGFftl*
"Darknet"	*bit.ly/2hSsme3*

WorldWideWebSize.com	*bit.ly/2hZ6OfH*
"The Deep Web: Surfacing Hidden Value"	*bit.ly/2hGB4hH*
The Big6	*bit.ly/2h0YZUN*
The SCONUL Seven Pillars of Information Literacy	*bit.ly/2ieoWBq*
NoodleTools	*bit.ly/2i9qFMw*
The Many Forms of Literacy	*bit.ly/2hTJnql*

Chapter 7: The New Creationism

"Library as a Kitchen"	*bit.ly/2iegaDs*
Shop Class as Soulcraft	*amzn.to/2ieoSl3*
A Whole New Mind	*amzn.to/2hTYlrs*
RTCO Tool Library	*bit.ly/2ieq5sK*
PNA Tool Lending Library	*bit.ly/2hGNh5V*
Berkeley Public Library's Tool Library	*bit.ly/2hZCLUU*

Chapter 8: The New Intelligent Design

The Metaphoric Mind	*amzn.to/2hU41qF*
"Mind Maps"	*bit.ly/2hSEUCm*

SparkFun: Analog vs. Digital	*bit.ly/2hbq6BF*
Stanford University: Institute of Design Reading List	*stanford.io/2hqb3zV*
The Third Teacher	*amzn.to/2havaGx*
The Atlas of New Librarianship	*amzn.to/2gZIA39*
National Center for Education Statistics	*bit.ly/2oo5fJT*

Chapter 9: Cool Tools

Cool Tools	*amzn.to/2hZDIN5*
NMC Horizon Report	*bit.ly/2h3Nufk*
Gartner Inc.'s Hype Cycle for Emerging Technologies	*gtnr.it/2iczwg9*

Toolkit of Physical Artifacts: Real and Physical Features Possible Within a Library

360-Degree Cameras	*bit.ly/2hX9hK4*
Animated Textiles	*bit.ly/2hepjju*
Augmented Reality	*bit.ly/2htdO3u*
Directed Sound	*bit.ly/2idbe5Y*
Egg Chairs	*bit.ly/2hth52M*
Folding Tables with Locking Wheels	*bit.ly/2hXJHVr*

Glass Wall Dividers	*bit.ly/2hXbRQv*
Greenhouse Mini	*bit.ly/2icAf17*
Hamsters	*bit.ly/2ihkH8a*
Digital Floors	*bit.ly/2i2NgGX*
Keva Planks	*bit.ly/2ihmRob*
LEGO	*lego.build/2i2NT3v*
Lighting	*bit.ly/2hVczLB*
Life-Size Cutouts	*bit.ly/2hVcNSX*
LittleBits	*bit.ly/2hVcV4M*
Musical Instruments	*bit.ly/2heB0X7*
Nimble	*bit.ly/2hbUPNv*
Phidgets	*bit.ly/2hVzZ3z*
Pillows and Cushions	*bit.ly/2hcdjwY*
Plants	*bit.ly/2htC59l*
RFID	*bit.ly/2hchWqW*
Robots	*bit.ly/2hckFkt*
Solar Power	*bit.ly/2hXFOQm*

Standing Desks	*bit.ly/2id8ntC*
Ultra-Ever Dry	*bit.ly/2hJEikk*
Wacom Tablet	*bit.ly/2htOPNv*
Walden Zone	*bit.ly/2hf7TTP*
ZSpace	*bit.ly/2hckJ3m*

Toolkit of the Ideational: Concepts or Ideas to Adapt and Try in a Library or Classroom Setting

AI in libraries	*bit.ly/2hcsRkq*
Appy Hour	*bit.ly/2kSDWa1*
Authors online	*bit.ly/2i3OrWQ*
Big History Project	*bit.ly/2h4loiV*
Blogs	*bit.ly/2htPXRp*
Book trailers	*bit.ly/2idzdSs*
Brain Rules	*bit.ly/2i3Mh9L*
Chrome Experiments	*bit.ly/2hJPTzU*
Content-curation tools	*bit.ly/2idBFIF*
Digital libraries ranking	*bit.ly/2i3VhM2*
E-portfolios	*bit.ly/2hY48Sp*

FutureTimeline.net	*bit.ly/2hfnhiN*
Genrification	*bit.ly/2hXRUZY*
Human Library	*bit.ly/2hJTVrS*
"Imbecile" and "Moron"	
Infographics	*bit.ly/2iidTHx*
Learning Commons	*bit.ly/2iig6m5*
Learning Theories Map	*bit.ly/2hY8TLt*
Library Views	*bit.ly/2hJZeru*
OCLC	*bit.ly/2hSzlq4*
Padagogy Wheel	*bit.ly/2hVUUnd*
"Play Is Hard Work"	*bit.ly/2hXVNOe*
"The Power of Play in Learning"	*bit.ly/2hfiHkT*
"Remix Creators"	*huff.to/2hW0mX8*
Libraries Trending Now	*bit.ly/2hu2iVG*
Visualization Methods	*bit.ly/2i43bF9*
Visualization Periodic Table	*bit.ly/2h4EU04*

Chapter 10: Wait, I Never Signed up for This

The Atlas of New Librarianship   *amzn.to/2gZlA39*

Chapter 11: Marketing Is Essential

"Reach of Leading Social Media and Networking   *bit.ly/2heeFYo*
Sites"

Chapter 12: The Third Teacher

"Is the Library the New Public Square?"   *bit.ly/2ilikkG*

On Looking   *amzn.to/2hhZzCK*

Concordia University: "5 Ways to Design a School for *bit.ly/2hwOTMz*
Brain-Based Learning"

The Language of School Design   *bit.ly/2ihBVGu*

"Campfires in Cyberspace"   *bit.ly/2hi6c83*

The Atlas of New Librarianship   *amzn.to/2gZlA39*

"Classroom of the Future"   *bit.ly/2heBn2n*

"33 Educational Design Principles"   *bit.ly/2ihFhJD*

"Indoor Environmental Quality of Classrooms"   *bit.ly/2ilr8Hx*

Toolkit for Learning Spaces

BREEAM	*bit.ly/2hxEMXW*
Green Star	*bit.ly/2imBM0i*
Learning Space Toolkit	*bit.ly/2i1k9GQ*
Learning Space Rating System	*bit.ly/2hflHMr*
LEED	*bit.ly/2i1kSl4*

Chapter 13: Building a Smart and Intelligent Library

Smart Nation Platform (SNP)	*bit.ly/2imKn3p*
"50 Sensor Applications for a Smarter World"	*bit.ly/2i8U7yT*
"Corning Ware Projection Screen"	*bit.ly/2hPaZwY*
Multiple Intelligences Quiz	*bit.ly/2imTtgf*
"Designing Classrooms of the Future"	*bit.ly/2hPtalV*

Chapter 14: We Are Storytellers

Frames of Mind	*amzn.to/2hyfrx3*

Toolkit for Finding the Best Books

Amazon	amzn.to/2hZKVgs
Booklists by Age	bit.ly/2hZMj2N
Booksource	bit.ly/2i1T3Q2
Common Sense Media	bit.ly/2h931uh
Cool Tools	bit.ly/2hfRRXX
Goodreads	bit.ly/2hPqVPv
Lexile: Find the Right Book for You!	bit.ly/2h93BYZ
LibraryThing	bit.ly/2ingeAQ
Literature Map	bit.ly/2hZJ8ld
Mrs. ReaderPants	bit.ly/2hfTMw0
OCLC WorldCat Genres	bit.ly/2hfUY2o
Shelfari	bit.ly/2hPqVPv
What Should I Read Next?	bit.ly/2i1QPQQ
Wikipedia: Great books	bit.ly/2hZPbwm
YALSA's Book Awards	bit.ly/2h98TEa

YA (and Kids!) Books Central	*bit.ly/2hjwAyp*
Young Adult Books in Series and Sequels	*bit.ly/2hZO93L*
YourNextRead	*bit.ly/2hfWRf*

Toolkit for Book Awards

Agatha Awards (Mystery)	*bit.ly/2i9oYLB*
Bailey's Women's Prize for Fiction	*bit.ly/2hRkXO6*
Bram Stoker Awards (Horror)	*bit.ly/2hjBlb5*
Caldecott Medal	*bit.ly/2hyk0r9*
Christy Awards (Christian)	*bit.ly/2hZMdYM*
Culinary Classics Awards (IACP)	*bit.ly/2hPzU3p*
Edgar Awards (Mystery)	*bit.ly/2inaDL4*
Hugo Awards (Science)	*bit.ly/2hjynDH*
Indie Bestseller Award List	*bit.ly/2i9u7Dm*
International Horror Guild	*bit.ly/2hys4lg*
James Tiptree, Jr., Literary Award (Science)	*bit.ly/2h8WnUY*
James Beard Foundation Awards (Culinary)	*bit.ly/2hZMevQ*

John W. Campbell Memorial Award (Science Fiction)   *bit.ly/2ioVHvO*

Lambda Literary Awards (LGBT)   *bit.ly/2ib15Du*

Macavity Awards (Mystery)   *bit.ly/2hzNdBZ*

Man Booker Prize   *bit.ly/2ilQx82*

Mystery Writers of America (Mystery)   *bit.ly/2hzNbtV*

National Book Awards   *bit.ly/2haCvRf*

National Book Critics Circle Awards   *bit.ly/2ioKTh4*

Nebula Awards (Science Fiction and Fantasy)   *bit.ly/2i0ZGQ5*

Nero Award (Mystery)   *bit.ly/2i116tR*

Newbery Medal   *bit.ly/2haryiR*

Nobel Prize in Literature   *bit.ly/2hh24DR*

PEN/Malamud Award for Short Fiction   *bit.ly/2i3ns0s*

Pulitzer Prize   *bit.ly/2haoHXc*

Quill Awards   *bit.ly/2i14EfK*

RITA Awards (Romance)   *bit.ly/2hzP9KP*

Shamus Awards   *bit.ly/2hgWd1g*

Spur Award (History and Western)	*bit.ly/2ib3ZYU*

Toolkit for Ninjas

"25 Ideas to Motivate Readers"	*bit.ly/2hhMRCj*
Arts & Letters Daily	*bit.ly/2hAFJPn*
Fandom	*bit.ly/2hlC5Na*
Google Books Ngram Viewer	*bit.ly/2i1KYZ7*
Library Book Face's Photos	*bit.ly/2imVfCs*
The NounProject.com	*bit.ly/2hblsig*
PrintWhatYouLike.com	*bit.ly/2hlzlzl*
Readers' Advisory for Youth	*bit.ly/2ipNlOZ*
Reading Ladders	*amzn.to/2hlD5kp*
Reading Promotion Ideas	*bit.ly/2i1LZ3l*
TodaysMeet	*bit.ly/2hhzTVh*

Toolkit of Book Recaps

60second Recaps	*bit.ly/2hat4pQ*
Booknotes	*cs.pn/2hFVZBm*

CliffsNotes   *bit.ly/2hXXnge*

CrashCourse   *bit.ly/2i869Mh*

Chapter 15: Counting on Logic

"Sphero Challenge" video   *bit.ly/2hSMcrQ*

Toolkit for Logical/Mathematical Intelligence

AWW   *bit.ly/2hbg1Ql*

Chibitronics   *bit.ly/2i45Mls*

The Curiosity Box   *bit.ly/2ibX0yZ*

GeoGebra   *bit.ly/2in8JhA*

LittleBits   *bit.ly/2hVcV4M*

Scratch   *bit.ly/2hlLxA4*

Thingiverse   *bit.ly/2i1Ptmu*

Tickle   *bit.ly/2i1UGe8*

Tindercad   *bit.ly/2hhGYVC*

Wolfram Alpha   *bit.ly/2i1M7jr*

Toolkit for Hour of Code

"Angry Birds" with Code	*bit.ly/2in4Ucb*
Coding with Scratch	*bit.ly/2luuvkq*
"How to Teach One Hour of Code"	*bit.ly/2ineE6b*

Toolkit for Logical Stuff

Abacus	*bit.ly/2hhTR29*
Chess	*bit.ly/2inmj4s*
Checkers	*bit.ly/2hALYCu*
Curriki	*bit.ly/2i21mcl*
Khan Academy	*bit.ly/2hAGlo5*
Paper models	*bit.ly/2icaWsP*
Quantified Self	*bit.ly/2hSlHlb*
String Art Patterns	*bit.ly/2ic7qhX*
WikiHow	*bit.ly/2iq1i4O*

Chapter 16: A Sound Perspective

Frames of Mind	*amzn.to/2hyfrx3*

library@esplanade NLB	*bit.ly/2l582tf*
SAS Middle School Library: "Pachelbel's 'Canon in D'"	*bit.ly/2ipWFbg*
One Degree North	*bit.ly/2hSQ4Ji*
Clint Randles, University of South Florida: "Why Music Lessons Need to Keep up with the Times"	*bit.ly/2i49ZW0*
SAS Middle School Library: "Hobo Guitar"	*bit.ly/2lutkkZ*

Toolkit for Music and Sound

28 Records	*bit.ly/2i2aPQH*
Arpeggios	*bit.ly/2iq6Nk1*
Booktrack Classroom	*bit.ly/2hAX5eF*
Cassette Tape	*bit.ly/2hB0quv*
Chords	*bit.ly/2hbBgBj*
Chrome Music Lab	*bit.ly/2iq6Nk1*
Free Music Archive	*bit.ly/2i25tFf*
Free Soundtrack Music	*bit.ly/2i216K5*
Harmonics	*bit.ly/2hbzRuR*
Jamendo Music	*bit.ly/2iq5CBh*

Kandinsky	*bit.ly/2ipWYTg*
Melody Maker	*bit.ly/2i1YXy9*
Oscillators	*bit.ly/2inuC0b*
Piano Roll	*bit.ly/2hAZgiF*
Rhythm	*bit.ly/2i4ohWl*
Spectrogram	*bit.ly/2hARjtA*
Sound Waves	*bit.ly/2hIYRV8*
Strings	*bit.ly/2inATsA*
Theremin	*bit.ly/2inHpzK*
Voice Spinner	*bit.ly/2i4qLV5*
Free Music Archive	*bit.ly/2i25tFf*
Free Soundtrack Music	*bit.ly/2i216K5*
Jamendo Music	*bit.ly/2iq5CBh*
Theremin	*bit.ly/2inHpzK*

Chapter 17: Just Picture It

A Whole New Mind	*amzn.to/2hTYlrs*

Toolkit for Visual / Spatial Intelligence

3-D City	*bit.ly/2iq4ayE*
Canva	*bit.ly/2i2g6rA*
Copainter	*bit.ly/2i2dOZk*
DollyZoom.js	*bit.ly/2iqel0R*
Google Cardboard	*bit.ly/2hSWk3B*
Gush	*bit.ly/2hhW91b*
House Configurator	*bit.ly/2iq5At8*
Internet Graffiti Board	*bit.ly/2hATr4M*
Just A Reflektor	*bit.ly/2i27dOS*
LEGO Build	*bit.ly/2hbv1O0*
motionEmotion	*bit.ly/2hB4r1O*
Oimo.js	*bit.ly/2icL2VB*
Painter Bot	*bit.ly/2hSMYol*
Quietube	*bit.ly/2hhX2GU*
SceneJS	*bit.ly/2i232T5*

SculptGL	*bit.ly/2iq3NnN*
Slides Carnival	*bit.ly/2inDOS7*
Stop Motion Studio	*apple.co/2hASx8o*
TubeChop	*bit.ly/2hm3iPF*
Video Notes	*bit.ly/2hi0DEW*

Chapter 18: Let's Get Physical

Frames of Mind	*amzn.to/2hyfrx3*
Naperville Central High School	*bit.ly/2i2aqOd*
"Why Not Even Exercise Will Undo the Harm of Sitting All Day"	*bit.ly/2hSRZ0n*
American Diabetes Association: "One Minute and Forty Seconds of Walking"	*bit.ly/2iclfMl*
Illinois Public Health Institute	*bit.ly/2icKgll*
"Brain Rule 1"	*bit.ly/2hbKjTa*
"Brain Rule 8"	*bit.ly/2hT5FbA*
The New York Times	*nyti.ms/2hBa5AU*

Chapter 19: Listening to Mother Nature

Naturalistic Intelligence   *bit.ly/2hi6F8L*

Jane Goodall, PhD   *bit.ly/2iqq7hh*

Chapter 20: Know Thyself and Others

Frames of Mind   *amzn.to/2hyfrx3*

Quiet   *amzn.to/2i77rnh*

Toolkit for Introverts

Human Library   *bit.ly/2hJTVrS*

Personality Tests   *muse.cm/2hoiiN6*

Virtual Counselor   *nbcnews.to/2hdXK4K*

The Human Library   *bit.ly/2hJTVrS*

Chapter 21: Virtually There

Shakespeare, "As You like It"   *bit.ly/2isZTLd*

James Gee   *bit.ly/2i6UaxW*

Jane McGonigal   *bit.ly/2hor8dl*

Toolkit for Game-Based Learning

Institute of Play	*bit.ly/2hofQGn*
Scheller Teacher Education Program	*bit.ly/2i6TxnU*
OpenAI	*bit.ly/2ir19Cx*
Peacemaker	*bit.ly/2ifpVC4*
Quest to Learn	*bit.ly/2he063R*
TensorFlow	*bit.ly/2hooWmc*
Meron Gribetz	*bit.ly/2i791s7*
Isaac Asimov	*bit.ly/2homhJz*
The Inevitable	*amzn.to/2hkwbKu*
Library of the Future	*bit.ly/2hDWBoI*
"Virtual and Augmented Reality Will Reshape Retail"	*bit.ly/2hW24K9*

Toolkit for Virtual and Augmented Realities

Google Arts & Culture	*bit.ly/2hE8yu0*
Google Cardboard	*bit.ly/2itcBcQ*
HoloLens	*bit.ly/2ifmyLz*
Oculus Rift	*bit.ly/2ifsc01*

HTC Vive	*bit.ly/2hVSR4t*
Meta 2	*bit.ly/2isZMz1*
The Singularity Is Near	*bit.ly/2hanSlY*
The Telegraph	*bit.ly/2i7fa7F*

Toolkit for Artificial Intelligence

"2016 Will Be a Pivotal Year for Social Robots"	*bit.ly/2i5JUnm*
"Brain-Computer Interface That Works Wirelessly"	*bit.ly/2hX7kNn*
Human-Computer Interaction Resources	*bit.ly/2hlnbEW*
Reactable	*bit.ly/2i5I063*
WowWee Rovio Robotic WebCam	*amzn.to/2hlpQP6*

Chapter 22: Phoenix Rising

Winning	*mzn.to/2hXdZaG*

Chapter 23: Just Do It

"7 Best Survey Tools: Create Awesome Surveys for Free!"	*bit.ly/2hXaYHa*

Chapter 24: Forecasting the Future

KnowledgeWorks.org	*bit.ly/2hlrosf*

KnowledgeWorks: "Learning System of Year 2025" *bit.ly/2heZquR*

ALA: Center for the Future of Libraries *bit.ly/2hu2iVG*

"Hype Cycle for Emerging Technologies" *gtnr.it/2iczwg9*

Horizon Report *bit.ly/2h3Nufk*

Chapter 25: Paradigm Shift

"The Hollow Men" *bit.ly/2luxycq*

Acknowledgments

Before his move from Singapore, my good friend Doug Tindall said to me, "You need to write a book about this."

"Yeah," I said, "maybe someday I will."

"No, really," he said, "I have some contacts who can get you published."

Doug and I considered writing the book together since he had contributed so much work and thought into transforming our library, but he was heading off to a new job in the United States and didn't have time to work on this project. Nevertheless, I took his advice and contacted Holly Clark at EdTechTeam Press. Holly listened to my ideas, looked at some of my writing samples, and had the faith in me to draw up a book contract.

As a first time author, it was a huge relief to have the support of an experienced team with editor and book coach Erin Casey guiding me through the process. Many thanks to Erin and her team members Whitney Alswede, Annie Kontor, and Janalisa Soltis for the hard work they put in checking my facts, repairing my damaged sentence structure, and smoothing out the organizational flow. Thanks also to Genesis Kohler who designed the book cover. In the end, I am responsible for any errors or inconsistencies you may find in this book.

My sincere appreciation goes to the many individuals who have supported me, collaborated with me, and inspired me throughout my library career. After spending thirty-five years in education, I am preparing to retire from school work in two years' time. As such, this book brings some closure and a chance for reflection on my years as a librarian. Two librarian friends Charlotte Draper and Terri Rolfe gave me the encouragement I needed to enter the profession. Sarala Nair and Premala Sekaran provided valuable expertise in the early stages of my career. Juninah Latif and Paula Sivanandan taught me much of what I now know about library science. I want to thank my "thought Ninja," Mike Pelletier, my "thought Shepherd," Mark Boyer, and my SAS colleagues who partnered with me in the Connections Project. A special thanks goes to master craftsman James McMullen and his talented colleague Shahrin Aripin for transforming the SAS Middle School Library into its current incarnation and for continuing to create and support innovations in this cool setting. Thanks also to the SAS faculty, my library colleagues, and the creative students we work with for the great projects, ideas, and community spirit you bring to our library each day.

Finally, I want to thank my wife, Kate, and my daughters Emily and Alex for their patience, support, and understanding throughout this long and challenging process; I couldn't have done it without you.

*grafo*EDU

MORE BOOKS FROM GRAFO EDUCATION
GRAFOHOUSE.COM

Manejo del Salón de Clase en la Era Digital
Prácticas Efectivas para Espacios de Aprendizaje Ricos en Tecnología
By Patrick Green and Heather Dowd

The Spanish-language edition of the popular book Classroom Management in the Digital Age helps guide and support teachers through the new landscape of device-rich classrooms. It provides practical strategies to novice and expert educators alike who want to maximize learning and minimize distraction. Learn how to keep up with the times while limiting time wasters and senseless screen-staring time.

The Google Apps Guidebook
Lessons, Activities, and Projects Created by Students for Teachers
By Kern Kelley and the Tech Sherpas

The Google Apps Guidebook is filled with great ideas for the classroom from the voice of the students themselves. Each chapter introduces an engaging project that teaches students (and teachers) how to use one of Google's powerful tools. Projects are differentiated for a variety of age ranges and can be adapted for most content areas.

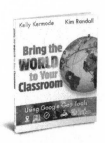

Bring the World to Your Classroom
Using Google Geo Tools
By Kelly Kermode and Kim Randall

We live and work in a global society, but many students have only a very small community or neighborhood as their frame of reference. Expand their horizons and help them increase their understanding of how they fit in the global landscape using Google Geo Tools. This book is packed full of how-tos and sample projects to get you and your learners moving forward with mapping, exploring, and making connections to the world around you.

The Martians in Your Classroom
STEM in Every Learning Space
By Rachael Mann and Stephen Sandford

In *The Martians in Your Classroom,* educator Rachael Mann and former Director of Space Technology Exploration at NASA Stephen Sandford reveal the urgent need for science, technology, engineering, and math (STEM) and career and technical education (CTE) in every learning space. Proposing an international endeavor to stimulate students' interest in science and technology, they highlight the important roles educators, business leaders, and politicians can play in advancing STEM in schools.

The Spaces You'll Go
By Rachael Mann

What kind of careers might exist in space? Join the adventures of Cas and Kanga Blue as they explore the answer through a playful mix of astronomy and imagination. Children and parents alike will be inspired to dream bigger and aim higher as they visit planets, asteroids, and space stations, tagging along with the intrepid Cas and kangaroo-turned-robot Kanga Blue to learn firsthand about occupations that are literally out of this world. This lighthearted romp through seventeen space-related careers is designed to encourage children's interest in Science, Technology, Engineering, and Math, often known as STEM. But even more importantly, it is meant to empower kids to believe that they can do whatever they dare to dream.

About the Author

Ron Starker has spent thirty-five years working in education as a teacher, counselor, librarian, and consultant. He graduated from Lewis & Clark College with a bachelor's degree in psychology and education. After two years of teaching, he completed a master's degree in counseling and trained as a school psychologist at the University of Oregon. He worked as a school counselor, teacher, and testing coordinator in Oregon Public Schools and, later, as a school counselor in Brussels, Belgium, and Vienna, Austria. He earned his MLIS Degree at the University of Hawaii. Throughout the second half of his career, he has worked as a school library media specialist at the Singapore American School.